"I Was Content
and Not Content"

"I Was Content and Not Content"

Cedric N. Chatterley

and Alicia J. Rouverol

with Stephen A. Cole

THE STORY OF
LINDA LORD
AND THE CLOSING
OF PENOBSCOT
POULTRY

With a Foreword by Michael Frisch

With Photographs by Cedric N. Chatterley

With an Essay by Carolyn Chute

SOUTHERN ILLINOIS UNIVERSITY PRESS

Carbondale and Edwardsville

Printed in the United States of America

03 02 01 00   4 3 2 1

A previous version of a portion of Alicia J. Rouverol's essay, "The Closing of Penobscot Poultry," has previously appeared in *The Journal of Applied Folklore* 4.1 (1999): 5–21, © 1999 Hisarlik Press.

Library of Congress Cataloging-in-Publication Data
Chatterley, Cedric N., 1956–
    I was content and not content : the story of Linda Lord and the closing of Penobscot Poultry /
Cedric N. Chatterley and Alicia J. Rouverol, with Stephen A. Cole ; with a foreword by Michael
Frisch ; with photographs by Cedric N. Chatterley ; with an essay by Carolyn Chute.
        p. cm.
    Includes bibliographical references (p.).
    1. Lord, Linda, 1948– 2. Penobscot Poultry—History. 3. Poultry industry—Belfast—Maine.
4. Belfast (Me.)—Economic conditions. I. Rouverol, Alicia J., 1961– II. Cole, Stephen A., 1955–
III. Title. IV. Title: Story of Linda Lord and the closing of Penobscot Poultry
        HD9437.U62 C48   2000
        337.7'66493'092—dc21
        [B]   99-25059
        ISBN 0-8093-2237-4 (cloth : alk. paper)   CIP

The paper used in this publication meets the minimum requirements of American National
Standard for Information Sciences—Permanence of Paper for Printed Library Materials, ANSI
Z39.48-1992. ⊚

TO G. PHILLIP LORD
(1910–1992)

AND
RUBY H. LORD
(1913–1989)

AND THE
WORKERS OF PENOBSCOT POULTRY

Contents

Foreword

MICHAEL FRISCH

ONE OF THE MANY REMARKABLE THINGS ABOUT this remarkable book is how naturally it flows from its title. From its descriptive subtitle alone, you, the reader, can gather that the book is the life story of a woman named Linda Lord and that her story is somehow enmeshed in the closing of a factory named Penobscot Poultry. You don't need to know much more than that to plunge in, for you will quickly discover that this relationship—an individual's story set against the more general story usually indexed these days under the heading "deindustrialization"—is what this very unusual constellation of texts and images revolves around.

As the centerpiece, there is the individual life story itself, rendered in Linda Lord's own words. Then there is the world of Penobscot Poultry and Belfast, Maine, illustrated through Cedric Chatterley's striking photographs. Chatterley and interviewer Stephen Cole offer brief notes, and editor Alicia Rouverol and novelist Carolyn Chute, a former Maine poultry worker herself, provide essays that speak powerfully to Linda, to each other, and to us.

One of Rouverol's two scholarly essays provides a useful perspective on the Maine poultry industry and its decline, by way of exploring the broader issues of deindustrialization in many communities like Belfast. Her other essay is equally helpful in discussing what is so interesting and complex about oral history—about, that is, the relationships and processes through which Linda came to tell her story to her interviewers and, in effect, to all who read the book, many of us from far outside the world of Belfast, Maine. Carolyn Chute offers her own personal, passionate, and pointed commentary on working-class rural Maine—industry, community, and people—and on the obstacles to communication across class lines about this world. In characteristically in-your-face terms, she forces readers to confront the contradictions involved when one group of people becomes the object of the concern, interest, and sympathy of others. Recognizing the almost inevitably dehumanizing and problematic "consumption" this involves, she suggests, is absolutely necessary if we are ever to understand each other and what is common and different in our lives.

All this flows, as I say, quite naturally from the descriptive phrases of the subtitle. But what about the curious quote that precedes them, "I Was Content and Not Content," which is almost too easy to pass over once we hit the serious subtitle business announcing the content of the book? If the subtitle describes straightforwardly what the book is *about*, this title quote may offer the best clue as to what it is really trying to *say.* If so, it might be worth pausing just a bit to think about what this quote is doing here and why—and how the book flows from this part of the title, too.

To this end, I'll begin with a personal story that may seem a bit far afield—if the famous playwright Anton Chekhov and turn-of-the-(nineteenth)-century Russian aristocrats strike you as standing a long way from a Belfast, Maine, chicken factory.

A number of years ago, a friend dragooned me into helping fill out the community theater cast for a local production of Chekhov's great play, *The Three Sisters.* My role was that of Kulygin, a schoolteacher and the cuckolded husband of Masha, the most tempestuous of the sisters. I had little acting experience and needed a lot of coaching, a good bit of it involving how to deliver some crucial lines: In the face of every humiliation and disappointment that is his lot, Kulygin repeats, "I am content, I am content, I am content." The trick was to say these words in a way that was not merely pathetic but that also made clear how determined the man was somehow to keep going, to avoid the self-pity immobilizing the other characters in the play.

Those lines came back to me when I first read Linda Lord's words on the title page, and they stayed with me as I read on. The more I read, the more it struck me that, personal echoes aside, Chekhov and Linda Lord were speaking to each other in ways that help frame the material in this book.

Beyond poor Kulygin, *The Three Sisters* involves a family of fading aristocrats in the twilight years of a Russian nobility soon to be swept away by modernization and revolution. They are stranded in the provinces a long way from the center of power and sophistication in their world. "Moscow, Moscow, Moscow," the sisters sigh in their various ways. They, their lovers, and their friends spend most of four long acts complaining about boredom and bemoaning their fate. (I recall our valiant director's struggle, not entirely successful given our dubious talents, to keep a wonderful play *about* boredom from *being* boring, but that's another story.)

Linda Lord throws all this into sharp perspective. Here are Chekhov's nobility and aristocrats who despite all their wealth and privilege insist, in effect, that "we are not content." Here is Kulygin, the determined middle-class professional, who unconvincingly but poignantly insists, "I am content," when he so obviously isn't. And here is Linda Lord, a working-class woman from rural Maine, who when asked whether she was content in her job in the poultry industry resists and deflects the either/or choice by saying, well, "I was content and not content," and then goes on to offer her story in her own way. Hers is a telling statement, and it is a telling choice to place her declaration on the title page. Here are some of the things that choice tells me:

By beginning in this way, Linda's story goes on to illustrate that working-class people may not fit the obvious categories others so often use to engage and measure them, whether these be categories of middle-class values taken as self-evidently universal, or categories of academic analysis assumed to be somehow deeper or truer than what people can know as they reflect on talk about their own experience. The place to start, we are told, is by checking our questions and assumptions at the door—and approaching Linda's story on her own terms, to see how these can challenge and complicate, rather than be squeezed into, the world of our own assumptions.

I have some experience with the capacity of working-class narratives of industry and deindustrialization to do just that, having collected and published a series of life-history interviews with Buffalo, New York, steelworkers in the aftermath of the virtual evaporation of that region's once-mighty steel industry (*Portraits in Steel*, with photographer Milton Rogovin, Cornell University Press, 1993). In this work, I was repeatedly struck by how regularly my interview subjects moved around the convenient categories, frequently of an either/or nature, so often used to describe industrial work, family, and community before, during, and after job loss of this kind. They both liked and hated their jobs. They often identified with the union and/or the company, yet felt betrayed by either or both. They saw themselves as victims of the plant closings, yet refused to act or feel victimized. They were deeply nostalgic and yet fully involved in moving on. Even more to the point, they resisted the very notion that their lives were defined by their work situation, past or present, offering instead a more seamless web in which worlds of family, neighborhood, and community were woven together with work and workplace in their own identities.

My project focused on big-city workers in a grand-scale primary industry filled with romance and awesome power. Even though my interview subjects were far more diverse (including several women) than the conventional image of the brawny steelworker suggests, all were nevertheless shaped profoundly by the skill, drama, and scale of heavy work in steel and the communities around it. Perhaps still a bit intimidated by these qualities, I have to say I did not quite expect to find such similar patterns in Linda Lord's world—involving, as it does, a small factory in rural Maine, and work—especially in the "blood tunnel"—to which nobody, leastwise Linda herself, attaches anything close to romance or excitement.

This made it intriguing for me to realize how resonant was the view through Linda Lord's eyes and words. Her work at Penobscot, her sense of family responsibilities, community, and place, her interests in music (she plays in a country band) and motorcycles—all are intertwined, making the job loss and her response at once more and less complicated, more constraining and more cushioned. The dense weave of detail in Linda's narrative, especially as framed by the various commentaries, helps to underscore some broadly applicable insights reducible neither to the romance of steelmaking nor to the lack of romance of chicken killing, but grounded, rather, in the broader realities of working-class life in communities and a world in transition.

It seems to me these insights are best drawn out by readers rather than pronounced upon by commentators. In the case of *Portraits in Steel*, one of the factors that took me and my collaborator to some ten publishers before we were offered a contract for our project was our insistence on permitting readers to engage and learn from the narrative and photographic portraits directly, rather than treating these as so much raw material to be pushed through interpretive mills of our own devising. So I won't presume now to interpose my own take between readers and the rich encounter that waits in the following pages. But since I do come from the academic world, and since the dialogue between perspectives and vantages is at the heart of the texts that follow, perhaps I will claim one word—literally—in order to acknowledge "where I'm coming from" as directly as do Linda Lord, Alicia Rouverol, Cedric Chatterley, Stephen Cole, and Carolyn Chute.

I first encountered some of this material as a respondent on a scholarly panel at the Tenth Berkshire Conference on the History of Women, held in Chapel Hill, North Carolina, in the summer of 1996. Our session, "When Plants Shut Down," included a paper by Alicia Rouverol that featured generous drafts of Linda Lord's words and Cedric Chatterley's photographs. The panel as a whole spoke directly to the conference's theme, "Complicating Categories: Women, Gender and Difference."

"The Berks" was a wonderful and exciting conference, but as with many academic congresses these days the air was pretty thick with theory and jargon—the kind of catchphrases that in every field serve as shortcuts to communication among those who know exactly what is being referred to but that can be impenetrable and oppressive to those coming from outside. Our panel was happily immune to this contemporary plague, so much so that in my comments I suggested with tongue fully in cheek that we were buzzword deficient and that in order to be taken seriously by others we needed to coin a buzzword of our own. The word I offered, referring to a quality discovered in the several papers, the same quality I have been discussing here in my comments on the "content/not content" title, was *multivalence*, with emphasis on the second syllable, so as to echo but contrast with the word *ambivalence*.

Ambivalence, as generally used, suggests uncertain feelings or a confusion of values. But *multivalence*, I suggested, evoked the very different quality that we were hearing: multi-valents, many values, the holding of different values at the same time without implying confusion, contradiction, or even paradox. As in being "content and not content." Multivalence, as this book demonstrates and argues powerfully, implies a way of being in the world—one that, as I've been suggesting here, may be particularly characteristic of working-class experience, challenging and complicating our categories and asking us to think about things in very different ways.

I'll close by applying the point to the book as a whole, not just to the qualities of Linda Lord's remarkable narrative, in order to underscore just how outstanding it is in form and potential effect. There has been a long debate in oral history over the uses of interviews in and within "history." Everyone agrees that interviews can provide a great deal of otherwise inaccessible information, but that is pretty much the end of consensus. Many professional historians insist that these "data" need to be "handled with extreme care" and used only when confirmed by and within a broader range of historical tests. Others feel that such an approach involves an unnecessarily restrictive approach to truth—that what is important in oral history is as likely to lie in interview statements as windows onto the life experience, culture, and understanding of the interview subject. In this view, an interviewee is not just a source of "data" but rather one who through the act of relating experience functions as his or her own historian, making some sort of meaningful sense of experience.

For many of us, this approach suggests a combination of the two positions grounded in the simple observation that an oral history interview is a living dialogue—a dialogue about historical experience between people with often very different interests and approaches, but with a shared capacity to engage the meaning of the past, and each other, in the process.

What I find so striking about this book is the way that the notion of respectful but indispensable dialogue has been expanded beyond the interviews with Linda Lord to inform the entire project. The book is unusual, I think, in offering such a complex constellation of voices—including but not limited to the central protagonist and with no voice being specially privileged. The book offers the voice of direct experience as well as the voices of broader historical and analytic perspective, of direct hands-on observation and participation, and of critical observation from within the heart of the world the book presents.

The whole, in my view, is a lot more than the sum of the individually fascinating parts. And as a result, I'm sure that however "multivalent" in theme, there will be few readers left ambivalent about its real power. Like Chekhov in his world, Linda Lord and her colleagues address some central realities that define ours, raising the broadest questions from the soil of a very particular place and moment.

Buffalo, New York
July 1997

Acknowledgments

"*I WAS CONTENT AND NOT CONTENT*" BEGAN AS A modest documentation project conducted by photographer Cedric N. Chatterley and oral historian Stephen A. Cole. The project took shape initially as a traveling exhibit, "One Year Later: The Closing of Penobscot Poultry and the Transition of a Veteran Employee," which opened in Belfast in 1989 and toured the state of Maine for the next year. The exhibit, like the book, came to life through the support of a host of individuals and institutions.

We are indebted to our original sponsor, the Northeast Archives of Folklore and Oral History (now the Maine Folklife Center), especially director Edward D. "Sandy" Ives and associate directors Mary O'Meara and Pauleena MacDougall. Staff members Theresa Gaten and Lisa Redfern participated in everything from exhibit text production to exhibit site logistics to final report assistance. We also received valuable assistance from Beth Ward, Julianne Dill, Kathy Corridan, Matthew Sweney, Bethany Aronow, and Marie Maclachlan. All tapes affiliated with this project and their accompanying transcripts are on file in the Maine Folklife Center, South Stevens Hall, University of Maine, Orono, Maine 04469.

We also wish to thank the project's principal funder, the Maine Humanities Council, especially Dorothy Schwartz, Richard D'Abate, and Deborah Zorach, for supporting the original exhibition and underwriting some of the manuscript preparation costs. Humanities scholars included Sandy Ives; Richard E. Barringer, director, Public Policy and Management Program, University of Southern Maine; Paula Petrik and Richard Judd, Department of History, University of Maine; Carolyn Chute, author; Jay Davis, then editor of the *Waldo Independent*; and Bernard Lewis, owner of Penobscot Poultry. Many of these scholars guided the original exhibit, and their comments, suggestions, and exhibit opening lectures laid an essential foundation for this book.

Principal contacts and participants at each exhibit site should be recognized. At the Belfast Free Library: Doug McDonough, Jay Davis, Bernard Lewis, Richard Barringer, Paula Petrik, Carolyn Chute, and Stephen Cole. At the University Gallery, University of Maine, Machias: Paula Petrik and Bill Little. At the Katahdin Area Training Center in East Millinocket, Maine: Beth Mahoney. At Fort Western Museum/Maine State Library, Augusta, Maine: Jeff Zimmerman, J. Gary Nichols, and Paul Rivard. At Portland Public Library: Richard Barringer, Paula Petrik, and Kerry O'Brien. At the Hudson Museum, University of Maine, Orono: Richard Emerick and Paula Petrik.

Cedric Chatterley acknowledges the support of his parents, Jay and Dorothy Chatterley, and all the family, Susan Touchstone, John McKee, Erik Jorgensen, Mark Wethli, Alice Steinhardt, Jody Calderwood, Gary Kolb, Georgia Wessel, David Gilmore, Jane Williams, Betsy C. Nelson, Denver Butson, Rhonda Keyser, Greg Hershey, David H. Lanner, Patrick Ryan, Arlene Anderson, Robert and Esther Doherty, Anne Doherty, and Brian Schaffner and the staff at B & L Photo in Carbondale, Illinois.

Our text benefited from the advice offered by Jacquelyn Hall, Glenn Hinson, Della Pollock, and Michael Frisch. Other readers included Kathryn Nasstrom, Jill Hemming, Roberta Chester, Sandy Ives, Jay Davis, Archie Green, Bob Hall, and Thomas Dublin. Many thanks also go to Peter Coclanis, Jefferson Cowie, and Michael Montagna of the State Planning Office in Augusta, Maine, for reviewing the historical section, and Galen Rose, also of the State Planning Office, for helping secure statistics.

We received valuable research assistance from Laura Finkel, Fred Lloyd, Donna Carver at the Department of Poultry Science at North Carolina State University, Charlie Campo at the Bangor Daily News, and the librarians at the Maine State Library, Maine Historical Society, Portland Public Library, special collections and reference department of Fogler Library at the University of Maine at Orono (especially Jennifer Jack), and the interlibrary borrowing office and reference department of Davis Library at the University of North Carolina at Chapel Hill (especially Ridley Kessler). Rebecca Folger at the State of Maine Bureau of Corporations, Elections and Commissions also provided critical assistance.

We are especially grateful to literary agents Jane Gelfman and Nina Ryan and to Jim Simmons and Carol Burns, our patient editors at Southern Illinois University Press.

Carolyn and Michael Chute, Liz Brown, Bill Bamberger, Alice Boyle, Jill Hemming, Colin Austin, Lisa Napp, and Jack Bernhardt provided moral support. Alicia Rouverol especially wants to thank her husband, Lance Walker, for his support and companionship and her parents and family for understanding what this all meant to her.

Finally, we would like to thank (posthumously) Bernard Lewis for granting permission for the original plant tour and also Penobscot's workers for sharing their thoughts with Steve and Cedric and allowing Cedric to photograph them. We especially thank Linda J. Lord for her generosity and her commitment. We feel fortunate to have her as our collaborator and friend.

Photographer's Note

CEDRIC N. CHATTERLEY

ON A COLD AND CLEAR FEBRUARY MORNING IN 1988, accompanied by oral historian Steve Cole and a plant manager, I walked the entire length and width of Penobscot Poultry, photographing as much as I could, stopping only to wipe the steam from my camera lens or to change film. A week earlier, Steve and I had been given a one-day tour of the grain mill, hatchery, and poultry barns outside Belfast in the midst of a blinding snowstorm, but nothing could have prepared me for what I saw and heard during the three-hour tour inside the plant itself. People everywhere worked in a steady rhythm. They stood in narrow aisles and handled shackled chickens in various states of disembowelment. Steel crates rolled in and out of large, underlit rooms. A man dressed in rubber boots and rain gear pulled a high-pressure hose and sprayed down the well-worn cement pathways. The motion, the noise, the blood, and the stench stick vividly in my memory today.

When the tour ended, I drove the seventy-five miles back to Brunswick in a daze. That same day, Carolyn Chute would be giving a reading at Bowdoin College, where I was teaching at the time, and I wanted to meet her. I had read her book, *The Beans of Egypt, Maine*, a few months earlier—just before I learned I would be coming to Maine for what I thought would be a short time. I approached her before the reading and asked, "Are you Carolyn Chute?" (I mistakenly pronounced her name Shute.) She said, "Yes, but it's Chute as in chicken." Thus began a lively friendship that would eventually lead to her involvement in this project.

I returned to the plant a week later, on the day it closed, February 24, 1988. I wanted to see if I had missed anything. Nobody was available to escort me, so I walked around to the back of the plant and opened the door to the slaughtering area. I turned and saw Linda Lord for the first time, and realized I had somehow missed her the week before. She was surrounded by swirling upside-down chickens, bleeding as they circled past her on a chain-driven line. Blood was everywhere, and I nearly slipped and fell as I tried to balance on an opening in the cinder block wall. Noise from the nearby defeathering machine was deafening, but I called out to her when several empty shackles swung past. She called back, but the line filled again, and she quickly took her knife to what would be the last chickens to go through Penobscot Poultry.

It was only later, by pure coincidence, that Steve and I met Linda at Rollie's Cafe in downtown Belfast, just blocks from the plant. She spoke openly about the twenty years she had spent at Penobscot Poultry and explained how she had gone to work for the company soon after graduating from high school in 1967. After a half hour, we asked if we could meet with her again and conduct a formal interview about her work at the plant and her feelings about its closing. A week later, we met at Gallagher's Galley in her hometown of Brooks, Maine.

As time passed, I became increasingly interested in what Linda would do after Penobscot closed. There were few job opportunities in her home community, and I was convinced she would have to leave the area to find work—an assumption based on what I would have done. With Linda's permission, I continued to photograph her as she set about the job hunt. I also conducted taped interviews with her over the following year.

There were times I felt I had no business asking Linda about the daily grind of looking for work, pressing her about whether she planned to stay in the area. Yet she was always willing to speak openly about the challenges she was facing, and it became clear that her plan was to stay in or near her hometown. The photographs and edited text we've included here chronicle her life at that time, as it unfolded.

As strong as my memories are of the Penobscot tour, they don't compare to the strength of character I see in Linda. Her commitment to her family, her friends, and her community has left a lasting impression on me, and I thank her for her generosity.

Introduction

ALICIA J. ROUVEROL

WHEN PENOBSCOT POULTRY CO., INC.—
Maine's last broiler-processing plant—closed its doors on February 24,
1988, Linda Lord and at least four hundred other plant workers lost
their jobs. Less conservative estimates suggest that over one thousand workers were
affected throughout the county. Located in the coastal community of Belfast (pop.
6,200), Penobscot Poultry for many years was the single largest employer in Waldo
County (pop. 31,000), and its demise put a sizable percentage of the community out
of work. For the state of Maine, Penobscot's closing marked the end of a once productive and nationally competitive agribusiness. For the town of Belfast, the
company's demise signaled the end of an era as the state's "capital" of poultry processing. Already suffering from high unemployment, the town had few opportunities to
offer these displaced workers.

Penobscot's closing was not an isolated incident. Maine had long seen a decline
in local industries, and in fact the nation as a whole has experienced a significant shift
in its manufacturing base over the past few decades. Defined as a systematic decline
in manufacturing jobs, deindustrialization is occurring in all areas of the country, not
simply in the Rust Belt or in those areas commonly perceived as manufacturing centers. And blue-collar workers are not the only ones who have been affected by
"downsizing." White-collar workers have been dislocated as well. Men and women
everywhere have encountered the effects of this profound economic shift.

*"I Was Content and Not Content": The Story of Linda Lord and the Closing of Penobscot
Poultry* seeks to chronicle—through oral history interviews and photographs—one
woman's experience of a plant closing and her subsequent efforts to secure employment. It tells the story of Linda Lord and her response to a local plant shutdown. Most
studies of deindustrialization emphasize the economic impact of industrial decline;
few consider the social, human costs. What does it mean to lose one's longtime employer, and what are the consequences? How does unemployment affect one's health,
well-being, and spirits? What choices must the individual now face? Many displaced
workers consider leaving to find gainful employment, but for some—especially
women—migration is not a viable solution. And what, ultimately, does it say about
her sense of home and place if a woman decides to *stay*?

Linda Lord's story offers a firsthand account of an individual facing such fundamental questions. Born in Waterville, Maine, in 1948, Linda grew up in Brooks, only
ten miles northwest of Belfast, in a family that had long made its living in the poultry
industry. She took a job at Penobscot Poultry straight out of high school and remained

with the company for more than twenty years. She worked in all aspects of poultry processing, primarily in the "blood tunnel," where she finished off the birds that had been missed by the automatic neck-cutting device—a job held by few women. In a work-related accident, she lost the sight in her right eye and fought hard for a settlement. In 1984 she joined a strike for better wages and benefits. Single and self-supporting, she was thirty-nine years old when the plant closed. In part because she was the primary caretaker for her elderly parents, Linda's goal was not to *leave* Maine for a better job but to *stay*, ideally to find employment within a reasonable drive from her home—the house that had been her grandmother's home—in the heart of Brooks's town center.

Alongside Linda's story runs the story of Maine's poultry industry and specifically Penobscot Poultry. The raising of poultry in this country had been a home-based operation for more than two hundred years. By 1860, Maine's "chicken business" focused almost solely on egg production; the state's farmers shipped thousands of eggs to Boston yearly. By the 1920s, they were either selling chickens locally or hauling them directly to city markets by truck. The broiler-processing industry—the industry in which Linda worked—did not take off until the 1940s. After World War II, market demand for eviscerated poultry (chickens whose entrails and extremities had been removed "online") began to transform the industry, and local industry leaders turned from buying chickens and trucking them to Boston to slaughtering them on-site in facilities like Penobscot Poultry. By 1954, poultry was Maine's largest and most important agricultural crop. The industry peaked around 1971. Although Maine was only tenth in the nation in broiler processing at that time, Belfast called itself the "Broiler Capital of the World." Waldo County had long been the center of the state's industry; by 1971, two of the state's five remaining poultry processors, Maplewood Poultry Co. and Penobscot Poultry, were located in Belfast. For Belfast, chicken was indeed big business.

Al Savitz started Penobscot Poultry in 1949, when broiler processing in Maine was in full bloom. Savitz later sold out, but then bought the company back with financing from the Lewis family. Upon Savitz's death, the Lewises—father George and son Bernard—took over the business. A native of Poland and the son of a butcher, George Lewis had had a long career in fish and meat processing as well as in real estate. He became one of Maine's most prominent businessmen and philanthropists. When George died in 1987, Bernard succeeded him. But Bernard contracted cancer and closed down the company the following year. In less than fifty years, Penobscot—and Maine's poultry-processing industry as a whole—had risen, flourished, and fallen.

Most attribute the industry's decline to competition with southern markets, which offered cheaper labor, as well as to the high cost of shipping grain to the state. But other factors also contributed to the industry's failure: poor management, problematic governmental policies, and unsustainable loans. Some studies have argued that the industry might have survived if the grain predicament alone had been adequately handled. Others knowledgeable about the industry, and about Penobscot in particular, say that the younger generation of Lewises had no real interest in carrying the industry forward. Lewis admits that he shut down the company not only because of the family's ostensible loss of $5.5 million but also because of family pressure to sell or liquidate the company. Regardless of the reasons, the industry did fail or, as some critics claim, actually fled the state, presumably for more "business-friendly" environs.

Linda Lord's story and the story of Penobscot's closing brings into question the relationship of business to community, reminding us that businesses and communities are in fact integrally linked—or perhaps more accurately *should be*, as Linda's own testimony suggests. Her narrative makes plain that plant closings have particular ramifications for women workers. But Linda's experience also points to how individuals cope with change, hardship, and uncertain times to create possibilities where few exist. Perhaps most important, her story reveals some of the challenges and complexities that most human beings share. "I was content and not content," Linda says of her job at Penobscot, and this seeming paradox is central to Linda's story. What are we as readers to make of this and other seemingly contradictory statements Linda makes in her interviews? And what do Linda's reflections tell us about the nature of work and community, about the choices we face in our own lives, about the human experience?

This project began as a collaboration, grew and developed further as a team effort, and has finally concluded through dialogue. It is a book of many parts by many contributors. Readers may wonder why as coauthors we chose to tell *or retell* Linda's story from so many perspectives. What follows is the story behind the story: who contributed and why, and how those contributions influenced what readers will find in these pages. Our goal was to tell *Linda's* story, but there are parts of us here, too. Like any documentary project, the final product reflects all who shaped it. And in the end we, too, have been shaped or altered in the process. Partly Linda's story, partly our own, it might be said that this book is not only about work and community but also about *home*: about those who choose to stay and those who leave.

When Stephen Cole first phoned Sandy Ives and me at the Northeast Archives of Folklore and Oral History at the University of Maine, he wanted us to sponsor a modest photodocumentary project on Penobscot's closing. A recent "transplant" from Massachusetts, Steve now lived in Belfast, just blocks from Penobscot Poultry. Although a relative stranger to Maine, he understood the significance of Penobscot's demise. He and his wife, Lindy Gifford, had recently finished a National Endowment for the Humanities-funded oral history project on Massachusetts's cranberry industry. But in that study they looked back on an industry that had originated one hundred years earlier. Penobscot's closing was imminent, and its ramifications were immediate. Steve himself was between jobs, seeking employment in the area, and he knew from his own job search that Penobscot's four hundred plus employees would have a rough time after the plant closed. As an oral historian, he hoped this historic event would be documented as it unfolded. As a local resident, he wondered what this closing would mean for his new community: *What would it mean for a town the size of Belfast to lose its central employer? How would the community survive?*

The plant was to close in a matter of weeks. Together we secured a planning grant from the Maine Humanities Council, and then Steve set out to find a photographer. The Bowdoin College faculty member he had in mind was on leave, and Steve found Cedric Chatterley instead. That particular turn of events shaped the project in ways we would not realize for some time to come. An itinerant photographer, Cedric had come to Maine for the spring 1988 semester only. Like Steve, he was a newcomer to the state. Based in Illinois, he had spent the past three years documenting the story of a young man named Mark through photographs and taped conversations. Nineteen years old and struggling to control a seizure disorder—and to maintain a home and family life in Cairo, Illinois—Mark had asked Cedric to document his situation and bring it to wider attention. Precisely because of this previous work, Cedric's concern and interest were immediately piqued by Penobscot's closing: *How would these workers respond? Would they stay in the region, or would they be forced to leave their homes to find work elsewhere?*

About ten days before Penobscot closed, Steve and Cedric toured the hatcheries and the grain mill. A week later, they walked through the plant. Although Belfast photographer Richard Norton had photographed at Penobscot years before, Cedric was told by management that he was the first photographer in the plant's history to have full run of the facility.

On that first visit, amid the clatter of the chain-driven line and the steady motion of chickens on the line, Steve and Cedric managed to speak with several workers about their circumstances. Some were upset and angry about the plant's imminent shutdown; others were relieved at the possibility of gaining new skills through job retraining and eager to secure what they hoped might be better employment. Overwhelmed by the noise, the sights, and the smells of poultry processing, Cedric and Steve left the plant likewise uncertain whether Penobscot's closing spelled disaster or whether it might be a blessing in disguise. And they were just as uncertain about how to proceed with the project: *How might they capture these workers' predicament and bring it to public attention?*

Steve and Cedric first met Linda Lord on February 24, 1988, the last day of operations at the plant, and that chance encounter became this project's central shaping event. They met at Rollie's Cafe in downtown Belfast at Penobscot's closing day party, just hours after the plant shut down. Linda agreed then to a formal interview the following week, and the story she told them in that first interview became the cornerstone of this project.

Cedric in particular felt that Linda's experience surrounding the plant closing had just begun, and he wanted to continue to photograph her as she sought work in the area. Although committed to moving the project forward, Steve had a prior obligation to finishing his book on the cranberry industry. In his stead, and on behalf of the Northeast Archives, I agreed to help secure funds for the exhibit. At this juncture—although I had never entered the plant and had not yet met Linda Lord—I came on board to coedit and coproduce the traveling exhibit with Cedric. This shift, too, would later take the project in unforeseen directions.

We secured a major grant from the Maine Humanities Council both for an exhibit and for a series of public forums on Penobscot's closing in Belfast and across the state. With the encouragement of Dorothy Schwartz and Richard D'Abate at the Council, we enlisted the help of several scholars. The group evolved serendipitously, as we searched for people who were knowledgeable about Maine's history and economy or about Penobscot and the poultry industry as a whole. Historians Richard Judd and Paula Petrik and economist Richard Barringer provided advice on the exhibit text. Paula also encouraged Cedric—now continuing as oral historian on the project—to ask Linda questions about men's and women's roles in the factory, her work in a nontraditional job, and her perspectives on feminism. Paula Petrik and Dick Barringer went on to give lectures at the exhibit opening in Belfast and at several other exhibit sites in the state. Steve Cole invited Bernard Lewis—then in the hospital with cancer—to speak at the opening, so that he might address community members directly about the plant's closing. Cedric asked Carolyn Chute—author of *The Beans of Egypt, Maine*, *Letourneau's Used Auto Parts*, and *Merry Men*—to write and present an essay when he learned that she had once worked in poultry processing. We also invited Belfast journalist Jay Davis to participate, because he had written extensively on the poultry industry. These lectures were later excerpted for inclusion in the traveling exhibit and would eventually serve as essential resource material for writing this book.

"One Year Later: The Closing of Penobscot Poultry and the Transition of a Veteran Employee" opened on February 23, 1989, on the eve of the one-year anniversary of the plant's shutdown. Held at the Belfast Free Library, it was an electrifying experience. More than two hundred people attended, including former poultry workers and community members who opposed the plant shutdown as well as those who applauded it. The lectures were provocative; audience members argued with panelists and among themselves. Carolyn's closing lecture, "Faces in the Hands," a reflection on workers' lives in our culture, left the audience transfixed.

For the following year, Cedric and I toured the exhibit to five additional sites in Maine and organized small public forums modeled on the Belfast event. Our goal was to engage local scholars and audience members in discussions about the impact of plant closings in their own communities. In some instances, the industries had long departed; in other cases, such as in Millinocket, workers from the local paper mill had been hard hit by recent layoffs. Inspired by their narratives and especially by Linda's story, Cedric and I set out to prepare a manuscript, find a publisher, and obtain additional funding. Carolyn Chute agreed to serve as essayist and offered to expand upon her lecture at the Belfast opening. The Council came through with grant funds, and the book began to take shape.

I agreed to write the book's introduction. Like Steve and Cedric, I came to this project as an outsider, and my ten years in Maine had done little to change that status. Originally from California, I had spent the previous six years working in folklore and oral history with a particular interest in rural women's narratives, and I had recently interviewed several Maine island women. I wanted to get at what I saw as the heart of Linda's narrative: *Why had she stayed at Penobscot for twenty years? And how did home and family factor into that choice?*

My work on the project would eventually draw me into a closer working relationship with Linda. Cedric and I began to spend time with her and her father at Mr. Lord's home in Brooks. Linda would go out clamming in Penobscot Bay and invite us over for Sunday dinner. Afterwards, Mr. Lord would regale us with stories about the poultry industry and the other industries that had come and gone in the state. As I got to know Linda and her father, I came to understand the profound influence of poultry in their lives. And as I reviewed the interviews, Linda's commitment to family became more apparent. Several years later, after Mr. Lord's death, I recorded an interview with her about the project, and over the years we have continued to talk about the developments in her life. This final collaboration brought out aspects of Linda's story not originally covered in the earlier taped interviews—especially the role of community in her life—which has shaped the story we have told here.

"*I Was Content and Not Content*" comprises five distinct perspectives or "voices": Cedric Chatterley's photographs, Linda Lord's oral history narrative, Carolyn Chute's reflections, my own historical and oral historical essays, and Steve Cole's epilogue.

Photographs document the final days at Penobscot Poultry and Linda's subsequent job search. They also chronicle Linda's daily life and community events throughout the following year. In the "Photographer's Note," Cedric briefly describes his initial reactions to touring the processing plant and to meeting Linda and Carolyn. Like many photographers, he offers little comment on the images, preferring to let them speak for themselves. Although he does not say so in his note, Cedric has expressed mixed feelings about photographing the workers, his desire to show their dignity, and yet his overwhelming response to the environment in which they worked. No stranger to hard manual labor (he had worked on oil-well drilling rigs in California), he was still shocked by Penobscot's working conditions. (Poultry workers in North Carolina, where I now live, attest to worse conditions still.) Cedric perceived these men and women as imprisoned by their circumstances with few options remaining once the plant shut down. And his rather nightmarish vision of the plant and the workers' plight comes through in these images. His photographs of Linda, on the other hand, reflect his immense respect for her and the trust that they developed over the course of the project.

Interedited with the photographs are our interviews with Linda. Much hand-wringing went into editing these transcripts. Cedric and I opted to preserve much of the first interview, deleting only repetitions and extraneous idioms of speech. We tightened the subsequent interviews considerably. Although we kept the chronology of the interviews essentially intact, we collapsed some of the later narratives into earlier segments to spare the reader repetitions that did not add to or further the story. These photographs and text represent the heart of the book, a visual and textual narrative of Linda's experience at Penobscot and thereafter.

Following the text and photos are essays *about* the closing of Penobscot and Linda Lord's story. Carolyn Chute's piece, "Faces in the Hands," is an expanded version of the lecture she originally delivered at the exhibit opening. The essay is less a reflection on Linda's story than it is an assessment of the plight of blue-collar workers in this country ("plaid shirt people"): how they are perceived and treated, and ultimately misunderstood and disrespected, by white-collar workers ("pastel shirt people") and by the very leaders who are elected to serve and represent them. Carolyn wrote the essay in the spring of 1991, and we have opted to leave it as a historical piece, including her references to former presidents Ronald Reagan and George Bush and then Maine governor John McKernan. When I asked Carolyn if she wanted to bring the piece up-to-date, she said that she saw no real need to do so. As she noted, the politicians in office have changed. "But does that matter? Is there ever a difference? Aren't they all from the same distant planet?" As her statement implies, this essay is a biting, incisive critique. As a writer, Carolyn Chute has long written about working-class Mainers' lives. But in this piece, she recounts her own experiences in poultry processing and other factory jobs and the challenges she faced as a working and welfare mother.

Following Carolyn's piece are two essays. The first explores the history of the state's poultry industry, detailing the rise and fall of that industry and illuminating the reasons for its demise. In this piece, I pose the question as to whether the poultry industry *might have* survived. And in so doing, I ask fundamental questions about communities and businesses and their mutual interdependence.

In the second essay, I explore the nature of oral history, what it offers us as readers, and how we might analyze Linda's narrative in that light. I also examine the process of editing the oral history text and suggest how collaboration with Linda Lord altered the story we told. Finally, I highlight the book's fundamental theme of paradox, apparent in both Linda's and Carolyn's stories, and consider how that theme gave way to the multivoiced or polyphonic dialogue we have put forward here. As an examination of the practice of oral history, this piece has a more academic tone than other pieces in the book. After some deliberation, my coauthors and I finally agreed that a scholarly perspective on Linda's story *did* belong within this volume but that it should be granted its own section separate from the introduction, constituting its own "voice" within the book. Linda's story was rich enough to handle (and in fact demanded) a variety of mediums and interpretations: visual, oral, literary, and academic. The result, we hope, will be a dialogue, sometimes melodic, sometimes dissonant, and one in which we hope the reader will share.

Steve Cole brings our story full circle in his epilogue when he tells of his November 1996 visit with Linda Lord in Brooks, Maine. His piece sheds an ironic light on the changes in Belfast since Penobscot closed and what those changes mean for Penobscot's former workers.

"I Was Content
and Not Content"

Approaching Brooks, Maine, on Rt. 7. April 1988.

Interviews with Linda Lord

The following abbreviations have been used in the interviews:
AR refers to Alicia J. Rouverol; CC refers to Cedric N. Chatterley;
SC refers to Stephen A. Cole; and LL refers to Linda J. Lord.

March 1, 1988; Gallagher's Galley, Brooks, Maine

SC   Linda, were you born in Brooks?

LL   No, I was born up in Waterville at the old sisters' hospital. But I've always lived here in Brooks. . . . I went to my freshman year at Moss Memorial High School, and then they were building the area school up on Knox Ridge, and I started my sophomore year up there and graduated from Mount View [in 1967]. After high school I went right into the hospital for an operation, and I wasn't supposed to work for a year; and come September, I got edgy and I started working a short time over at the [Unity] hatchery before I went down to the plant.

SC   What did you do?

LL   I de-beaked chickens, sexed them, injected them, de-toed them, de-beaked them, you name it I did it. [laughs]

CC   What is de-beaking?

LL   De-beaking is burning part of the bill off so they don't peck each other as they get bigger. . . .

SC   And then you learned to sex chickens, too. We hear that's rather a specific and actually sort of hard-to-learn task. Did you like working out there?

LL   It was all right. It was a job. At that time I was young, and I wanted to stay close to home on account of my mom being ill. And I wasn't there very long before they transferred me down at the plant because things were getting slow. It was either they were going to be laying off, or I had a chance to go up to the plant. I had looked around for other jobs, and I figured, well, I had been working with the company, I'd stay with them. So I went down to Penobscot.

SC   Let me back up a little bit. Did you go to the hatchery to work initially because your dad had also worked in the poultry industry?

LL   My father had been a pullorum [poultry blood] tester for a good number of years with the University of Maine. He did work for Penobscot and at the time for Maplewood [closed 1980]. Of course, during the summers, I worked for him testing birds. So I got to know quite a lot. Of course, we raised birds, too; we had laying hens for Maplewood so I'd grown right up. But no, that wasn't why I went over to the hatchery. It was, at that time, that was just about the only place that was hiring, you know. And I wanted a job. I was getting edgy not doing anything, even though I was supposed to stay out a year and not even work.

SC   Did other people you know from Mount View also hook up with Penobscot for a job?

LL   Not too many, no. As a matter of fact, a lot of the guys in my class were wiped out in Vietnam. I think we lost four or five. And the ones that did come back were disabled or not with it or either freaked right out on dope, you know.

SC   That's a large number of people from one high school. Well, probably your graduating class wasn't all that large in the end.

LL   I think it was a little over—maybe like a hundred and twenty in our class. I can't remember now, but I've got it on the back of my diploma. . . .

SC   So they transferred you down to Penobscot. What did you start doing there?

LL   Transferring. That's hanging [poultry] from the "New York" room after the feathers have been taken off and they've gone through the foot cutter—they drop down to the belt. I was working on Line Two, which did big birds and small birds. . . . But I kept breaking the skin away from my nails and getting blood poisoning streamers going right up my arm, so that's when I signed up for the sticking job. And the pay was a lot better. At that time I was going through a divorce, so I was out to get as much money as I could to support myself.

SC   What specifically was your job then?

LL   Just putting the bird into the shackle going out on the eviscerating line, after the feet have been cut off. They drop down on a belt which came to you, and you just would put them in a shackle so they could go out to be opened up and their intestines drawn out, and get your heart and liver and so forth out of the bird.

SC   So it's rough on your hands. How do you think that caused blood poisoning?

LL   Well, you take that infection that would set in, even though you'd try washing your hands good. And eventually it would get into your blood system and pretty soon, if you didn't take antibiotics or something, you'd have red streamers going right up your arm. And you'd take what helped to cut the feathers so they would pick better—the solution they added with the water [to remove the feathers]—and you'd take it with the grease and stuff, and that would cause you more trouble and make your skin peel right off your hands, too. My hands now are even sensitive to hot and cold where I was transferring, and it's been a number of years.

SC   So how long did you do that?

LL   About four or five years, then I signed right up for the rest of the time to go right out sticking.

SC   Were there a fair number of other people who work on the lines who have had these kinds of problems?

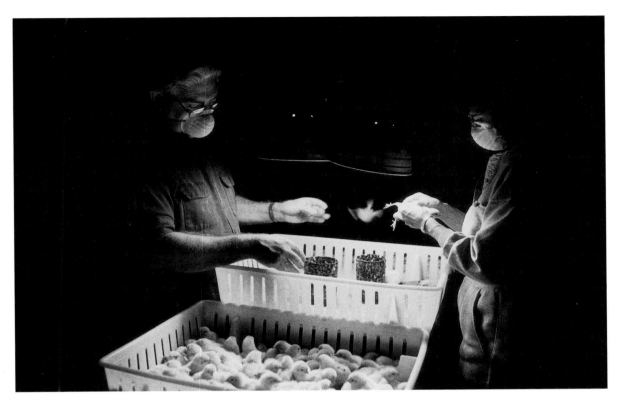

Husband and wife team "sexing" newborn chicks (up to 20,000 per day) at the hatchery near Brooks, Maine.

Poultry barn (capacity 100,000) near Brooks, Maine.

Trucks delivering live chickens to Penobscot Poultry, Belfast, Maine. February 1988.

LL   Everybody's had problems that's been there. A lot of people have had warts come out on their hands because of handling chicken. A lot of people have had tendinitis, you know. That work is hard work down there. And they've had blood poisoning, you name it. Or you get, well—what do they call it? You have like a rash break out all over you from the chickens, too, which eventually will blister right up with little pus sacks, and the skin will peel right off your hand, and they call it—"chicken poisoning" is what they call it. And I've seen people get it from wearing rubber gloves.

SC   Wow. Were you ever able to get any satisfaction from the company in terms of better conditions so that wouldn't happen? You had health benefits, right?

LL   Yeah, and if you had blood poisoning or anything, they'd send you right down to the hospital to try to get it cleared up. At that time they would put you on easy jobs until you either got over tendinitis or the rash on your hands and so forth. But as workmen's comp passed a few laws and stuff, then they had people just stay right out of work. They didn't want you even in there doing light work.

SC   Did that mean that if people had a problem, they were less likely to tell the company if that meant they now had to go home?

LL   A lot of people would stick it out and not say much. Because you had to be out over three days in order to draw on workmen's comp. If you were out maybe one or two days, you just couldn't get anything—you lost a couple days work. So a lot of people just kept going.

"Unloaders" stacking crates on a conveyor.

"Hangers" shackling poultry.

SC   So that job you had four or five years, and that's a total of how many years
      that you were at Penobscot?

LL   Twenty years in all with the company.

SC   Twenty years. So after that [transferring] it was into the sticking room or the
      "blood tunnel"?

LL   The sticking room, the "blood tunnel," or what I called the "hell hole," where
      they had so much blood. [laughter] No one wanted to come in there when
      you were in there. You were just by yourself until you got done work.
          When I first started out sticking, we didn't have any machinery in there
      then, except for just the stunners. And that first stunner that made the bird's
      head hang down is where we usually sat—two of us. There were two stickers
      in there and we had to do every other bird running right in a full line. And
      then about '79 . . . they were thinking about increasing the production down
      there. So they went into the sticking machines, which at first didn't pan out
      very good. But after a while, about a half a year, they got it straightened out so
      it would do a pretty good job. And then you had to back up the machine.

SC   So initially the stunner stunned the bird, but you had to stick them.

LL   Right. Grab it, take a knife and cut the vein right in by the jaw bone.

SC   So, by stunning, essentially that means that the bird was in shock?

LL   But not dead. The heart was still beating—just kept it kind of quiet. Then you had another stunner that would help to jar it again to get it pumping its blood out, so it would bleed out before it went into the scalder.

SC   How did that first stunner work? We saw it, but I wasn't quite certain how it operated.

LL   Okay, you had salt and water mixed together with electricity.

SC   So the bird's head ran over an area with salt and water?

LL   Yeah, and the head and part of its chest would run over that tray that had water and salt in it and the electricity going through it.

SC   So that would give the bird the shock?

LL   Yeah, and if you tried grabbing hold of it with your hand, you got quite a zap.

SC   I bet you did. So after the bird came to you, then another stunner got its heart pumping quickly.

LL   Pumping so it would pump the blood right out after you cut the throat.

SC   And that presumes the bird was dead.

LL   Yeah. And they figured the lines being stacked, it'd be all bled out before it went into the scalder and that way it [the bird] wouldn't be red.

SC   You know, the first day we photographed the hell hole, we were a little taken aback. It's a pretty gruesome scene in there. How did you feel about it when you began to work in there? . . .

LL   I was the type of kid growing up that nothing bothered me—blood or anything like that. So when I signed up for that job—of course I'd been in there and I'd watched and I had tried some, you know, on my breaks and stuff. . . . So I knew what I was getting into, and it didn't bother me, and I preferred working by myself than working by someone that might cause trouble for you on the line.

SC   How could people cause trouble for you on the line?

LL   Oh, throwing stuff, you know, not doing their bird, but trying to blame it on you. But at the end of it, they'd mark the shackle. . . . So they could tell just which one shackle it belonged to. . . . And if someone wasn't doing their job on a bird, they could trace it back.

SC   So you thought that maybe the disadvantages of working with other people were big enough that you rather would have stuck it out by yourself in that room.

LL   Yeah.

SC   It probably got pretty lonely in there, didn't it?

LL   Well, sometimes if they ran the line real slow you could get hypnotized. You had to keep getting up, moving around so you wouldn't fall asleep or something. It wasn't a very pleasant job, like in the summer it was real hot with all that rain gear and stuff on. And then in the winter, you just about froze to death before you got a good heating system in there.

The "blood tunnel" (guide bar and automatic neck-cutting device to the left). The back of Linda's head can be seen behind the board, top-center of the photograph.

Linda Lord at work in the "blood tunnel" on the last day of Penobscot Poultry. February 24, 1988.

Linda in the "blood tunnel."

Defeathering machine.

SC   Were the birds all pretty much dead by the time they got to you?

LL   No, they were still, you know, flopping their last flop before they died. That's why I was more or less, as you could see—with the rain kerchief, I was more or less covered right up so I wouldn't get too bloody. . . . The machine got, oh, maybe sixty-five to seventy percent of the birds, and the rest I had to do. . . .

SC   Did you make more money working in that job?

LL   Yeah, because that was top pay. I mean I got the same as the trailer truck drivers did. The last of it then was $5.69 an hour, which was more than what the people were getting on the line. Maybe five, ten, fifteen, or twenty cents more—because each job through that plant you had different wages. . . . The trailer truck drivers, or straight job drivers, and stickers and weighers got the same wages—$5.69 an hour.

CC   What was it paying when you first started working at Penobscot?

LL   When I first went in there, maybe like $3.25, $3.75 an hour. That was way back in '67. [Between 1967 and 1988] we got up to $5.69 an hour. I remember one summer working there, I made $1.25 an hour working in the plant. That was before I was out of high school.

SC   And your wages were dependent on what the union could negotiate, right? They didn't simply increase by ten cents every six months or something.

LL   No, every two years when we had another contract—whether we get a ten cent raise the first year, and maybe a five cent raise, or a ten and ten—whichever we could bargain on at that time and vote for it, is what we got. As far as

One of several singers to remove small hair and feathers.

Pin-feather inspector.

Workers transferring poultry from one conveyor to another.

The eviscerating line.

the cost of living was going up, it didn't help our wages go up, you know. We had that contract that we had accepted and that's what we got.

SC   Not a very strong union, or was it a strong, good union? Which would you say?

LL   I wouldn't really call them strong, no.

SC   There was a strike a few years back.

LL   Right, we were out on strike. . . . Must have been in about '84, I would say. I had to—I was a line steward—I had to go along. I didn't go for it at that time. To me, I figured the union was playing little cat-and-mouse games with the company, which almost cost us our chance of not getting back into that company. Because George Lewis, at that time, he had had it. We had a—what do you call it, a mediator or something. . . . It was just at a standstill, and a lot of people were getting hard up then and stuff. I did make a call to the mediator and talked with him and told him that a lot of people wanted to go back. . . .

SC   What was the crux of the issue? Was it higher wages? Was that the reason people went out?

LL   It was higher wages. They wanted us to pay for our medical bills and insurance and so forth and drop our wages at the same time. And, of course, the union people told us that we could draw unemployment and get food stamps. And people thought, well, gee, this is gonna be great, we have a vacation. I tried to tell them, you go strike you cannot get unemployment, you cannot get food stamps, and so forth.

      Well, they voted. After they voted down there in the hall at the Blue Goose and they found out a few things more, then they regretted the way they had voted. But we had to wait almost two weeks before we could go back and vote again about accepting the contract. We didn't have to wind up paying anything on insurance, but we had a $250 deductible—which for a married family, it hurt them quite a lot. Because that wasn't just on the whole family, it was on each individual. For me, where I was single, okay. It was only $250, you know, no sweat. I could probably pay it off in a short while anyway. But the married people, it really hurt because as far as the children, the wives, or the husband, it was $250 for each one.

SC   So how long was the union out on strike total?

LL   Two weeks.

SC   And when you came back, you had to accept the offer that Penobscot made at the beginning?

LL   Right. As far as I'm concerned, we lost more than what we gained being out on strike. We lost money, yeah. Not only that, but they hired what you call scab help coming in, which—the plant wasn't running that great. There was a lot of hard feelings there for a while, but we got back and people got their jobs back and they were happy, you know—even though we did lose a lot.

SC   They hired scabs from in town and around the area?

LL   Right, around the area. And people that they had fired before at Penobscot and were never hired back, they hired them back as scab help.

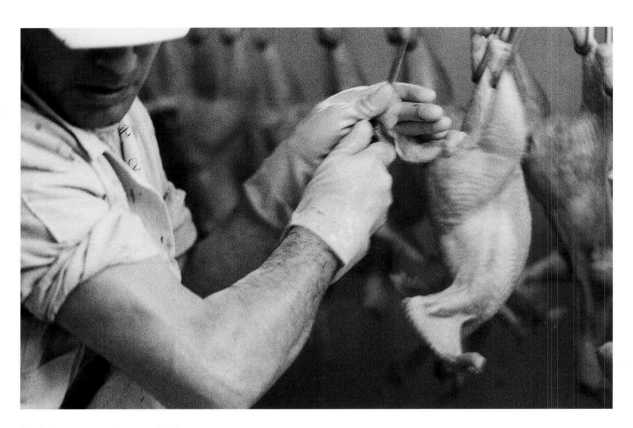

Final inspector cutting away bruises.

The eviscerating line.

Holding tanks of inedible poultry parts to be taken to the rendering room.

Penobscot Poultry, Belfast, Maine.

Workers on "Line One."

SC   You folks had set up picket lines there every day?

LL   Right. Yeah, each day we each had different hours that we came in, so that there was someone right there twenty-four hours a day. And there was some damage done to trailer trucks that came in and so forth, but I didn't go for it. I tried telling the people, keep your nose clean and say what you want to on TV, but don't do damage because it's only hurting us. And they had pulled out pins from on the trailers and the guy pulled out and the whole load dropped down and stuff. And he came out with a bat, and I just told the people, I said, "Get out away from here." I had a pretty good idea who did it, but I wouldn't say anything, you know. I said, "You're only hurting yourselves. Let's try to keep this clean and hope we can get our jobs back."

CC   So when you went back to work, did you make any more money at all?

LL   We got a ten cent raise the first year, and then I think it was another ten cents the second year. [According to an article in the *Maine Times* (30 March 1984), the workers received a sixty-five cent raise; however, they had taken a fifty-six cent pay cut previously. So the ten cent raise Linda is referring to takes into account the earlier pay cut.] But it didn't make up for what we lost in the two weeks we were out. And the way the insurance went, too, it—you know, we lost a lot. . . .

CC   So the insurance was actually worse after the strike?

LL   It was, yes. . . .

SC   Would you say the benefits at Penobscot were pretty good based on—

Worker in vending area.

LL   They were for a while until the laws and, of course, the cost of insurance stuff made it harder for the company to try to pay for all of this.

SC   When you folks were out on strike, what were George Lewis's reasons for not being able to give the union what they were asking for?

LL   The major reason was what it cost to raise birds here. You see, it cost a lot more up here than it did down South. So you can't give the people as much money, really. I mean, he claimed he had a margin that he had to go by. He knew what he could and couldn't do—and if we went for higher wages and stuff, there was no way that he could keep running and make ends meet and make money.

SC   I don't think we ever asked how much of a raise the union was going for during the strike.

LL   Oh, they started out with a dollar, but you know, you kept going and negotiating, it kept coming down maybe like 50/50 or 20/20 or 25/20. It wound up being what the company offered us was 10 and 10 [ten cents per hour the first year and ten cents per hour the second year on a two-year contract].

SC   Right. [pause] What would you say about most of the folks you work with at Penobscot if you were to describe them as a group?

Packaging on the further processing line.

Employee lunchroom.

LL   The majority of them were people that never had much of an education or didn't get through their education, okay. Some of them couldn't even hardly sign their names or make out an application form. Then you had some people that were a family, they had completed their education, who were fairly smart. But it was fairly good wages and close to home and they worked there.

SC   How would you describe yourself? Where would you put yourself in those groups?

LL   I regret the way things started out after graduation, having that operation and stuff. If I hadn't had to go in for that operation, I probably would have gone to college, okay. And like I said, my momma had been ill for a long time. She had one bad heart attack after the other. And then she wound up with a stroke and being paralyzed. So I more or less figured, well, you know, I was making fairly good money. I was able to save money. I stuck it out for that reason—to be close to home for my father. But now I regret that I haven't furthered myself as far as education.

SC   Would you say you were discontent, though, during the years you worked at Penobscot?

LL   I really wasn't happy. When I first went to work there, my hands were awful sore. They would swell up. You'd go home and you'd soak them and try to get so you could move them. And about when you got up in the morning so you could move your hands, you were back in there and you had to go through it again. Oh, it might take two or three months, and finally your hands get used to it. But it was a job. It was a fairly good paying job for around this area at that time. So, in some ways, I was content and not content.

SC   What would you say about most of your fellow workers there? Do you think they were content or discontent?

LL   A lot of them were because, like I said, they didn't try to better themselves in high school and so forth. So I mean they were content as long as they had money. Some of them would go buy beer, or the family people could support their family and get by—you know, it was all right.

SC   Did a lot of men work there who had a wife and kids that they were trying to support on a Penobscot Poultry income?

LL   Yes, there was a lot of them, quite a few. Up and downstairs, both [further processing and the slaughtering area, respectively].

SC   What about by age? Would you say the majority of the people there were middle-aged or younger, or did it vary a whole lot?

LL   I would say there were more middle-aged and older people in their fifties and near their sixties than there were the real young. The young people you couldn't keep in there. This day and age, young people they don't know what work is. They don't want to work. They figure there's so much welfare and stuff that they can draw on and stretch it for all it's worth.

      We had a lot of people that would just come in and right out the door; might not even stay a couple hours, because they didn't know what hard work was. See, I was brought up on a farm. I've always had to work hard all my life,

Further processing, second floor.

so as far as putting in a hard day's work, it didn't bother me. But a lot of these younger people that are just standing on the corner, hands in their pockets after they got out of school days, they don't know what hard work is.

CC So they'd come in and maybe work a day or two?

LL A day, or maybe a couple hours, and out the door they went. They didn't want any part of it.

SC And I suppose a lot of these middle-aged folks, like you, had put in a good number of years at Penobscot?

LL Right. And some had put in longer years than I had, maybe thirty or thirty-five years. I know one woman that pin-feathered in the New York room—she had in thirty-five years. And she raised her family on what she earned there at the plant.

SC That's a long time to work anywhere. It really is.

CC Have those people talked to you about how they feel about the plant closing?

LL We all felt bad. I mean, after a while I guess it was just like home, right? You've got your friends that you associated with each day. Now I didn't associate with that many, but a lot of people knew me. I had a few that I was very close with that were good people, you know. . . .

SC Pretty good crowd overall, you'd say, among the workers, or did it vary a lot?

LL They all got along fine as far as working. There might have been a few fights on the lines and so forth. But a lot of them, once you were outside the plant, it

Bagging roasters.

Workers on the cut-up line.

Hallway outside the lunchroom.

was a different story, because they knew they couldn't fight in the plant. There was a rule that they'd be automatically fired. But a lot of them were pretty roughneck; I mean they were brought up in barrooms. But your family people that were married and stuff, they usually went home and they minded their own business. . . . But as far as people working together, you know, the majority of people usually got along fine. If there was any real problem, if it was related to work, then that's when your line stewards and your chief stewards stepped in with the union people to try to get it straightened out before it got too far.

SC   If problems developed on the line, was that because someone wasn't doing their job, and so it made problems for people further on down the line?

LL   Mostly the machinery wasn't working right, okay. And they just kept pushing people and expecting them to do their top job, you know. And if the machines weren't working right, you couldn't get the production that you were supposed to get.

SC   So that meant that management would come down on you?

LL   Right, and then in order to try and get it straightened out, or try to get the machinery straightened out, it might take maybe a half a year, or a year, you know, and you went along that way. It would just make it hard on the working people.

SC   How were the managers there?

LL   You had some good ones and you had some bad ones. . . . But you had a few there—I won't name them—but they were just out to see what they could get off of women. And if you didn't put out, then they made it rough, tried to get—fire you.

SC   So they tried to make demands on you. Try to see you after work or something?

LL   Right, yeah. I had trouble with one foreman when I used to come in and set up in the morning. Because I'd be in there at four o'clock in the morning, setting up one whole line, getting ready for seven o'clock. I had one that gave me quite a hard time—tried to see me fired. But it didn't work. I stood my ground. We had the top people in from the company, argued it out. He was supposed to not harass me and leave me alone. . . .

CC   You said you'd go in there at four o'clock in the morning to get things started. Tell us about that. I mean, what would you get started?

LL   Okay. Like, I had all of Line One. I was hooking up the pipes, made sure the shackles weren't bent, machinery was running and so forth, and put machinery in its place. You know, just made sure everything was put together for when the line started at 7:05.

CC   And if you showed up at four o'clock, then what time would you get off work?

LL   When the rest of the line got done. Whether it was three, four, five, six o'clock.

CC   And would you get paid for the—

LL   I got time and a half for overtime. Anything over eight hours, I got time and a half. . . . And I used to come in on weekends and do a lot of painting and stuff, too, or maintenance work on the lines. Because they knew that I could—you know, they trusted me as far as coming in and getting the work done. They could rely on me. I wasn't one to miss much time. . . . Where I was single, I was out to get all I could make to support myself.

SC   How were the Lewises as owners? Do you think they were generally pretty concerned about the place and about the people who worked there?

LL   George was, and I think Bernie was until he came down with this cancer. . . . And I think that's one reason why he [Bernie] decided to fold up the plant, was on account of his health after he lost his father in May. [George Lewis died in May 1987.] George was very concerned; a lot of things he didn't realize were going on. And when we got to negotiating and I would bring up—I said, "You know, George, who was supposed to let you know what's going on here in the plant and how things were run?" Well, there was certain people in the office who were supposed to make out a report and let him know what's going on—which they were making it look good on paper, but it actually wasn't happening there in the plant. It got so that George himself was coming in maybe once a week, twice a week, whenever he felt like coming in every week, to find out just what was going on. He'd talk with the people. He really took an interest in trying to keep the place going. He was in his eighties then. . . . And George would try to make short cuts and things to make things easier for people, too. I mean, he'd come right down and watch people working on the lines and so forth, seeing if there wasn't some way to make things a little bit better so he could get a better production, too, when he found out he wasn't getting things on paper the way they were supposed to be.

Worker weighing boxes.

Linda and coworkers taking a break during the afternoon of the final day.

Two of Linda's friends in the lunchroom near the slaughtering area of the plant. February 24, 1988.

CC   When did you start to sense that Penobscot was going to close?

LL   When George Lewis died, a year ago May. I know his boys didn't want it when we were negotiating on new contracts all the time—the only thing that kept it going was George. . . .

CC   We've heard quotes saying that they haven't made a profit but only once in the last seven or eight years.

LL   There's probably been a few years that they haven't made money, because the market was down so low, I mean, because they almost overran the market with birds. I figured if President Reagan had stepped in like he has on a lot of these farmers with growing cabbage or so forth, if he'd put a freeze to the amount of birds that could have been put on the market and kept the price up, then everybody down South and up there [Penobscot] would have been happy.

    But down South the labor was cheap. . . . The southern markets would overrun, overpopulate the market. So the more birds that were put on the market, the price would drop. And, of course, when the market would drop, it would hurt us up here because it cost us more to raise birds. We had grain we had to ship, electricity, and transporting birds, and so forth. I mean, our farms were probably farther away [from the plant] than a lot of the farms down South. . . . And we didn't have as many diseases as they do down South.

SC   I've noticed in newspapers constant advertising for places like Perdue, though. I'm not sure I've ever seen any advertising for Penobscot Poultry.

Clean-up.

Hosing down.

LL   Perdue went all out, but he had the money to advertise, right? If you had taken Penobscot, it would have cost you millions of dollars to advertise. George Lewis figured it was better to put it in your production, your machinery and stuff, than advertising. And we had sales people going around—up in Canada, and all over the state of Maine, maybe Vermont and New Hampshire—that were trying to sell chicken. You had I don't know how many people, maybe three or four. They were out on the road all the time to try to sell chicken.

SC   They'd visit supermarket chains, places like that?

LL   Right, places like that. See, we lost a good contract with the Canadian people on account of feathers. They had one shipment of rotten birds sent, which lost a very good order, which hurt Penobscot. . . .

SC   What about the Maine supermarkets? Did Penobscot supply the Maine markets?

LL   Right, a lot of the stores in Belfast and Waterville and around, you could see Penobscot chickens in the supermarkets.

CC   How far would they ship from here? Would they go to Boston or—

LL   I've seen Boston and New York that they've sent birds out. . . .

SC   You know, in the Belfast papers, in the [Waldo] *Independent* and the *Republican Journal*, it was funny to read the letters to the editor about the closing of the plant. Some people in town seemed happy it was closing, and other people seemed disturbed. Did you ever get any sense that Belfast didn't want Penobscot Poultry there?

LL No, I think the majority of the store owners wanted to see Penobscot keep going, because it was going to hurt, okay, as far as them making money. There were a few that didn't want it on account of the feathers coming down through the city. The company eliminated a lot of that problem by putting a canvas over [the trucks], so you didn't get as many feathers or you didn't get the smell from cooking chicken stuff. The company did a lot about keeping trouble down as far as with the city, you know, and the waste and so forth from the birds.

SC Do you think if we were to ask most of the young people who worked at Penobscot whether they thought it was going to be better for them after the closing or worse, what do you think they'd say? People like you who have a good number of working years ahead of them?

LL It's going to be hard to say, because I really haven't had a chance to look around. Probably if it kept running, I would have stayed there and I'm sure the majority of the people would have, you know. Because it was a job, they knew five days out of the week, they were bringing home money. Now as it is, we don't know what's going to happen—whether we're going to better ourselves, or get a job that's not going to pay as much. As far as insurance, we don't know. I mean, everything is up in the air until we go through this workshop that we've got to go through and see just what they're going to offer us [Coastal Economic Development Corporation (CED), which offered job retraining].

SC Now no one has health insurance, at least from Penobscot?

LL Well, we were allowed to keep on for eighteen months with this insurance, okay. I'm paying for it now, $58.64 a month. . . . And married people have to pay over $100—I think it was $145—to keep the insurance going. And they wanted to take it right out of our severance pay. And I said, "Look, I don't want it taken out of my severance pay." If I find a job, then I might want to drop it. . . . In the meantime, maybe six months down the road, I might find a job that's got good insurance. . . . But I kept it just in case something happens and I wind up in the hospital, I've got insurance. . . .

SC Who do you think will be hurt worst amongst all the workers? Is there any one particular group that's going to have the hardest go now that the plant's closed?

LL It's the people up in their late fifties and early sixties that are going to have the hardest time trying to find something. But they claim they had a special program for those people, but a lot of them never signed up. They didn't have an education. I mean, they'd had to go on and get their high school diploma in order to further on with training, and a lot of them didn't want to bother. They said they'd been out of school for so long . . . that it wasn't worth it— that they need a job.

SC The two women that we were sitting with at Rollie's last week—

LL What we call Alex and then Jennie. They have signed up for the shoe place down there, the sardine place and frozen food [Penobscot Frozen Foods, Inc.]. But they haven't heard anything yet.

Foreman standing next to a window overlooking Penobscot Bay.

SC So are you keeping in touch with them?

LL Yes. Like every morning we sit together and have a cup of coffee and donuts, you know. And they were the two people I was the closest with down there. . . . Jennie, she lives in the trailer park across the river there in Belfast. And Alex, she lives down in Searsmont, and her daughters worked here. One daughter works here in the restaurant, and the other one works up at the hardware store, so it's a matter of twenty minutes away, cutting down through the back roads to where she lives. And she was in here the other day, Alex was, having supper with her daughters.

SC Do they have anybody they have to support other than themselves?

LL No, Alex just lost her husband a little while ago. So she's by herself now. She's got one daughter living with her, which eventually is going to be moving here in town because she works at the hardware store. Her other daughter lives down in Swanville there. . . . But her [Alex's] family is all grown up, so she's just got herself. And Jennie's family's all grown up, so she's just got herself, you know.

SC If this were a wish list and you were able to wish for where you'd be and what you'd be doing, let's say, a year from now, what would you say if you had your choice? . . .

LL I told you I was on the Brooks ambulance, and I would like probably to get into the medical field—something like that, a job that isn't going to fold, right? Of course, when I went to that meeting they had when unemployment was there . . ., I wanted to sign up for practical nursing, but they wouldn't even talk to me until I signed up for CED. But I would like—I think, the medical field where I've had so much background. And it's a good field to get into, because it isn't going to be something like Penobscot that eventually is going to fade out. There's always going to be sick people.

SC   How did you end up on the ambulance squad here?

LL   Due to my mother. I took the first responder course and the EMT course and so forth, where she had so many heart attacks. Matter of fact, one time she was having a heart attack, I was just taking that course and had to do CPR on her. And I was just starting to learn CPR, but I brought her to, got her to the hospital. That was before the Brooks ambulance got [started]—see, we put that together by ourselves; it didn't come all stocked and so forth. And because her health was so bad, I figured I better learn all I can. And I enjoyed it. Like I said, blood or anything doesn't bother me.

SC   So are you a certified EMT?

LL   Yes. As a matter of fact, I'm going back to take my refresher course. . . .

SC   Because then potentially, you could work on a squad around here somewhere?

LL   Right. Or anywhere. I know Kennebec Valley [Hospital], they were hiring EMTs. But that's quite a ways for me to travel. And they paid there—this is all volunteer around here. We don't get paid. We do get paid our meals if we're out on a run.

CC   Would you consider moving to Kennebec Valley if you had to?

LL   If I had to, I would relocate, because I've got to start looking out for myself now. And you know, I've got a brother that lives right up behind—he worked at the grain mill. And I've more or less got to start looking out for myself now instead of my family, you know.

CC   Is your mother still living?

LL   My mother is still living, but she's bedridden. They live right up on Route 7. My father is, what?—he's 77, so he's getting right up there in years. I think he worked until he was 67, because they couldn't find anybody to replace him at the University of Maine. See, he worked a couple more years after he was supposed to retire.

CC   How far is Kennebec Valley from here? If you had to move, how far would you have to move?

LL   Oh, I imagine it's maybe a hundred miles, if not more. I never really looked up to see where it is on the map. I know it's down country somewhere. [laughs] You're probably talking an hour, an hour and a half, maybe two hours at the most. So it'd be quite a lot to try to travel it back and forth, you know, every day.

CC   Would it be better pay than Penobscot?

LL   It didn't quote as far as what the salary would be. They were just sending out the flyers, if you were interested to contact them. But I never checked into it because at that time Penobscot was still going. Just before Christmas they sent that. That's before we got news the plant was closing. . . .

SC   What were people's reactions when you found out? That was, what, the Tuesday before Christmas that the news came out?

LL   I think some of them kind of surmised something would happen once George passed away. But they were still hoping that the place would still keep running. But then like I said, when Bernie's health got bad. Myself, I worked like a bugger all summer long because I had a feeling that the place was going to close, because I knew Bernie was really sick. And I was working seven days. I was working upstairs 'til eleven, eleven thirty, and just coming home and getting maybe two or three hours sleep before I was back in there. Then weekends I was caponizing. Caponizing. That's a male bird, you take the— what I would call the balls—out of a male bird and make them bigger, okay, get a fatter bird. They're like a rooster, but they're bigger, more meat on them and so forth.

SC   Where were they doing that? At the Unity hatchery?

LL   No. When the chickens were about maybe two and a half to three weeks old, we went into the farms and did them right there.

SC   So you were storing up for the hard winter ahead? Your idea was that it was going to—

LL   Right. I had a feeling that the way things were going down there—you couldn't get anything fixed, as far as machinery—that something was going to happen. And I told a lot of people, I said, "You'll be lucky if you ever see another contract." Our contract would have, I think, expired March 25, along there some time. It was just that feeling right along the way. Bernie was sick, George passed away.

SC   What do think will happen to the plant? Do you think it will be torn down and they'll build condos there?

LL   I've heard condos. I was talking with Bernie the other day. He looked me up to shake my hand and, you know, congratulate me for being a good worker and a faithful worker and so forth—which, you know, he really went out of his way. He didn't have to. I mean, one worker is just like another probably to him. But he did know me. Like I said, I was on the negotiating team quite a lot as far as contracts. And I asked him, I said, "You know, Bernie, what do you think is going to happen?" And he said, "As far as I know, I'll probably wind up selling the machinery and so forth." But he said, "You never know, there might be a buyer. It'd surprise me just as much it would the people that worked here." And there are still people looking at the place and looking at the grain mill and looking at the hatchery. So you don't know, really. But I've heard that they're interested in buying Penobscot and making condominiums.

SC   Was your brother laid off at the grain mill?

LL   No, he'll be there until after June, I guess. He was more the head honcho over there at the grain mill. And he told Bernie he'd stick by him 'til the end. But there's been talk that the grain mill might be bought. And if it is, he'll probably be staying there, because he knew how to mix up the grains and so forth

Workers returning smocks on the final day of Penobscot Poultry.

and run the computers over there. But he can step out, because he's had two years at MCI [Maine Central Institute] at Pittsfield and then he had five years at the University of Maine. He went back to get a master's degree in something. . . . He's got the education behind him so he can probably step out and get another good job somewhere. Where I didn't further my schooling, so that's why if the schooling will offer anything, I want to try to better myself. . . .

CC   If you were going along and getting what you wanted out of that [further schooling] and Penobscot reopened, which way would you go? Would you go back? Would you continue your schooling?

LL   If I figured that my schooling would eventually better myself and better pay, I would go that way.

SC   And not return to Penobscot?

LL   No. Because the way I look at it now, the chicken business here in the state of Maine is just about phased right out. Because it's costing too much for us, for the grain to be shipped. You have to pay electricity, you have to pay the fuel. You know, it's a sad thing really, because it's put a lot of people right out of work. And it's just due to the cost of living. No, I'd probably continue with my [schooling]—because they'll still pay your unemployment. . . . So I'm going to get by. You know, I'm going to pay my electricity bill, telephone bill, whatever bills are coming in. I'm going to get by, plus be getting the schooling—so I'd be a fool to pass it up.

SC   You'll have twenty weeks of severance pay, each paycheck equaling one week's

A line-worker and foreman embrace before leaving on closing day.

salary at Penobscot, and then jointly with that unemployment while you're—

LL   Unemployment, and this week I'm getting my vacation pay, which was four weeks. So that's going to amount to about $800. I'll get about $6,000 severance pay.

SC   And then unemployment while you're in training?

LL   And I won't have to go around looking for a job, either, as long as I'm going to school. And that means quite a lot, because each week when you sign up for unemployment, you've got to have at least three places that you've been— their names, telephone numbers—if they want to see if you've been in there. It's a lot of red tape to it. . . .

CC   You say you work here [at the restaurant] part-time?

LL   Help out, yeah. Wash dishes.

CC   Are these friends of yours?

LL   Friends, very good friends. . . . They came from New York, so I showed them how to get by here, you know. There's a lot of things that they didn't have to do in New York that you have to do here. Like yesterday, I came down and I helped him flush his hot water system and his pressure tank and stuff. . . . I showed him how to clean that, which he never had to do in New York. In return, when I was working, he kept my wood stove going. So we've kind of looked out for one another and done favors. And that's the way a good friend should be.

CC   Are you going to work today?

LL   I'll work tonight, yeah. For a while they had a girl that was coming in days, and there was a while I thought, well, I'd work noon and night. But then, with the schooling and stuff, I figured it's better to keep it at night and let this other girl make some money, too. . . . And it'll give me a chance to help him out here, you know, plus study. So I don't know how far I've got to travel or anything like that. I won't know until I go through this workshop. . . . There's quite a few people that signed up. Now, this afternoon I got to go down and sign up for unemployment at the Legion Hall.

CC   This is in Belfast?

LL   In Belfast.

SC   You'll probably see lots of folks there.

LL   Probably. Because they say that some are to go in the morning and then a bunch go in the afternoon, and then they're going to be there tomorrow, too. I've got until from 12 to 3 that I'm supposed to be in there to sign up. . . . My father is going, because I've got to stop and go in the safety deposit box. I've got to get my divorce papers and stuff, so I can put a freeze on my pension plan through the union. I've got to show that I was born, my birth certificate, and I've got to show when I was married. . . . There's more red tape, I'm telling you. You should see the different forms I've got to fill out. Almost have to sign your life away.

CC   You say you're remarried now?

LL   No, I'm not. I'm single. [laughs] No, I had enough the first time.

[As the interview comes to a close, Linda and Cedric discuss plans to meet in downtown Belfast. The recorder is turned off while they talk. Cedric and Steve begin to discuss work-related accidents, and Linda mentions that she lost the sight in her right eye while working at Penobscot. Cedric turns on the tape recorder in midsentence.]

LL   —It pitched me right into the guard that they had go over the foot cutter, pitched my head right—I hit right up through here and it broke the skin. I still have scars.

      It was two or three days later that I started seeing bright light in this eye. . . . In another three or four days, I was in the hospital. Stayed there a month and a half, and had three operations on that eye. They got the retina fused on, but they couldn't get it to lay down so I could see anything. They almost sent me to Boston.

CC   How did it happen again?

LL   I hit my head on the chain guard to the foot cutter on the Number One side in the New York room. It hit right up through here—. See, when that hose— it doubled up and caught on the leg, and then when it let go it was just like elastic. And I had on that rain kerchief, instead of wearing a hard hat. I had on that rain kerchief and it tore that right—you know, a freak accident. . . .

CC   Did you get any compensation for it?

LL   It took three years to settle it, but I got something. But it wasn't, you know— $13,000 will not bring back your eyesight or anything like that, you know.

SC   Did they at least cover the cost of the operations and stuff?

LL   Well, my insurance I had with the company paid, and I had a balance of $2,000 or $3,000 left that I had to pay, right? And I had filed with workers' comp, right? Because you had thirty days then, and like I said, for two or three days I didn't realize what I had done until I started seeing stars—that retina started ripping from the top and peeling right down like wallpaper.

And so I made out the claim and stuff. The union people wouldn't pay me my weekly indemnity where I filed on workmen's comp, and workmen's comp wasn't going to pay anything—because, see, when I was little I got shot with a BB gun, but I still had eyesight in that eye, right? So they were trying to say it was a sickness and, oh, give me a hard time. So it took three years to settle it.

And, finally, the union people came across and started paying me my weekly indemnity while I was out, because I didn't have any money coming in. It was a good thing I had a lot saved up in my checking account and stuff, or I'd been hurting. But finally the union people paid and then after three years, after workmen's comp settled up and stuff, they [the insurance company] paid. But when I called up the nurse and I said, "What do you want me to do with this balance of $3,000?" And she said, "Pay it." And I said, "Well, you may have shit on a lot of people down here, but," I said, "I'm not dumb enough to let it happen to me." Because they did play some awful things on people to try to get out of paying, and that's when I started getting the workmen's comp lawyers in there to talk to people and find out what the people could do and not do. So I got the union people and they hired a workmen's comp lawyer for me—it didn't cost me a cent. It took three years to settle it and I don't know how many court hearings, but I finally got something out of them. . . .

Yeah, they made a settlement and stuff, but it wasn't enough to pay for— you know, when it interfered in your trying to get a better job. I looked around for other jobs when I was working down there at Penobscot, but a lot of places they wouldn't even talk to you if they knew that you had one eye, because they just didn't want someone like that around. I don't know why, the people are doing a job and stuff. It doesn't affect your judgment or your distance or so forth, you know. Of course, now I'm a little careful, I've got one eye to go me the rest of my life, so I take precautions. I don't ice skate, I don't ski like I used to. . . .

But like I said, it wasn't enough to pay for the loss of an eyesight.

SC   At least you got them wise to—

LL   It educated a lot of people down at the plant just what they could get as far as working. . . . If people had chicken poisoning and stuff and were out because their hands were so raw, workmen's comp covered it, and a lot of people didn't realize that. See, and I told my lawyer just what was going on down there at the plant and what they were pulling—what they tried pulling on me. Each year they had workmen's comp lawyers come in and talk with people, just what they could draw—you know, different injuries, what it would cover and so forth.

CC   The union had the—

LL   The union didn't—it was up to me; I told them. The workmen's comp people came in just to represent the people. Of course, I told the union people, too; they didn't realize what was going on. Because a lot of them [the workers] weren't smart enough, like I said, to even sign their names, so they wouldn't fight it. But when that nurse tried it with me, she was in the wrong, and when someone's in the wrong, then I'll really fight for my rights.

And I looked out for a lot of other people down there, too. Because when I was a line steward and an assistant chief steward, I figured the people were in the right and the company was in the wrong, and I really went all out to fight for them, you know, get what they needed.

CC   So people would just get blood poisoned and then stay out for a week or two?

LL   Stay out and they'd just lose out on a week's wages and, you know, they didn't realize they could draw on workmen's comp. The company wasn't going to tell them, because that was that much the company didn't have to pay on—it upped your insurance, you know. It was a wonder I didn't lose my job over that. But if they'd have tried to fire me over that deal, I'd have gone right to

Linda signing up for unemployment benefits for the first time in her life. American Legion, Post 43, Belfast, Maine. March 1, 1988.

Augusta to the Labor Board, and I think the company would have had one heck of a lawsuit against them.

CC   Oh, yeah.

SC   Good thing you worked at Penobscot.

LL   Like I said, I'm no dummy. I might not have as much education as some people who have gone to college, but at least I know where I stand with the laws and just what the company can do and what they can't do. Because I've had that much training.

[Cedric tries to pay for the coffee.]

LL   Don't worry about the coffee and stuff, believe me. You keep your money.

March 15, 1988; Rollie's Cafe, Belfast, Maine

[The tape begins in the middle of a conversation with Linda Lord about the Brooks Volunteer Fire Department. She is joking about someone who has recently backed the truck into the tight-fitting garage and scraped all the lights off the side of the truck. She says that, even though she has sight in only one eye, she backed the truck in three times on her first try without scraping anything off. The conversation switched to the high wages of UPS truck drivers—a job for which she had recently applied.]

CC   Did UPS say anything about the lack of one eye being a problem?

LL   No, as long as you can lift, they don't care. You stay there and work a year, you can bet on driving one of the trucks around—and that pays $16 per hour.

CC   That's three times what you made down there [at Penobscot]. Are you bitter now that you think back about your wages?

LL   Am I bitter? [pause] I didn't think we got paid fairly for the work that we did in the plant and how hard we worked, you know, and under the conditions. But what can you do? Like I said, a lot of times I did apply for jobs when I was working at Penobscot that maybe paid seven. But you figured by the time

Linda at Rollie's Cafe, Belfast Maine. March 15, 1988.

Linda and friends at the Brooks Community Park during a drill for the Brooks Volunteer Fire Department.

Taking a test for possible employment with Champion paper company, Coastal Economic Development office, Belfast, Maine. March 1988.

you traveled and every two years you had to have a vehicle—figured your insurance, gasoline, the whole works, and keeping the car up. It wasn't worth it—you know, traveling. So I just stayed there. And it was close to home. [long pause] I'll be all right. If I have to, I'll sell my house, you know. I could get some good money out of that. It's paid for.

CC   Is there a market for real estate up there?
LL   Prices are going like mad right there in the town of Brooks. Out-of-state people are buying them.

SC   Have you seen any other Penobscot people?
LL   Not too many.

SC   What are the folks doing, that you've seen, that are going through the same CED stuff you are?
LL   Well, I've talked with one, and she didn't complete it. She said it was just a waste of time. . . . I suppose by tomorrow we'll know more what's going on. . . . Oh, there's bound to be something come out in the paper, some more jobs that I'll be interested in. . . . Mainly I'll hit all the job service areas around—Waterville, Bangor, Belfast, Rockland—places like that. That'll be the next step I'll be doing.

SC   If there was a place in this area where you'd like to work, where would it be?
LL   I imagine if I could get some schooling, I'd be going into a hospital. Or if I

Linda on her front porch.

could get into Champion [International Corporation] over there, I wouldn't mind that, really, because the pay is good over there.

SC   What kind of stuff would you do at Champion?

LL   It's hard to say. Whatever they'll—one advertisement was a common laborer, the other one was some kind of a machine operator. But I can do anything if I put my mind to it. I'm the kind of woman that can climb, you know. . . .

  Well, life has never been easy for me. It's been one constant struggle. Whatever I wanted, I've gone after it and worked hard at it. That will be the same way here. But I will not go out to Fort Halifax [a poultry plant in Winslow, Maine, specializing in further processing]—even though it pays six dollars an hour.

CC   Is it the pay, or is it that you just don't want to do the work anymore?

LL   Well, I just don't want to work in a chicken place. I never did care for Penobscot, but I stuck it out because the pay was good—close to home. [pause] I'll see if I can't better myself.

CC   Have you been in other processing plants? Did you ever visit Maplewood? Were they more automated, or was the equipment any different?

LL   From what I talked with people there at Maplewood, they had a lot better equipment and everything ran a lot better than over here at Penobscot.

CC   I wondered about that. I guess this [equipment] is pretty outdated.

Kitchen table.

LL   A lot of this machinery's been there before I even went to work. They just kept patching it up. We did put in new scalders because the other ones were getting so paper thin that water was just about to go right through the sides of them. And I helped tear those apart—the old scalders. I helped put in the new scalders there in the New York room. We even put in new lines and stuff. That's about the only thing that's been done. But a lot of that other stuff has been right there, like the chillers. They did advance some on modern equipment, but it didn't ever replace anybody. That person still had to back up that machine. . . . Like the sticking machine I had on my side—it took him [the plant manager] a year to work on that, to get it so that it would work. Then I came up with a lot of ideas to tell him how to fix it so it would work. Because when it [poultry] came through, you couldn't adjust it. . . . We might work four or five hours on big birds and then there'd be small ones. You couldn't adjust it. So they had to tear that—so they could wind it up and wind it down, adjust the blade so it'd cut deeper in the big birds than the smaller ones. [long pause]

   Oh, I have learned something out of it [CED], I suppose. How to write out a resume, which I could do anyway—fill in application stuff, you know. If you don't want to answer it, just put "N.A." or "salary open." I always put in what I was getting there at the plant, you know. But I won't take less than what I was getting there [Penobscot], I'll tell you that. . . . When you sign up for unemployment, you can refuse a job that pays less, too. You don't have to take it.

CC   Is your unemployment coming in yet?

LL   Yeah. I received my first check last Friday. It was dated back to the first week of March. See, they hold back a week on you, just like they did to you at Penobscot.

CC   And you're getting your severance pay, too?

LL   Severance pay should be coming this week. . . . I'm drawing $161 a week [unemployment], because I put in so much overtime there at the plant, see. I grossed a lot more than a lot of the other people did, so it helped. . . . I know I was putting in 60–65 hours in the summer—close to 70. . . . See, I'd come in and I'd start at four o'clock in the morning, and it would be eleven or eleven-thirty before I got out of there at night, because I went upstairs packing out [further processing], whatever they wanted me to do up there. So I mean I was putting in some good hours, but the government was taking it out of me, too. . . . And I got my vacation pay—they took out over $300 right out of me. I had just had my income tax made out. I had to wind up paying $277 to the state, $43 to the federal. And I had extra money taken out of me.

CC   It's because you're single and all that nonsense. . . . What would you do when they gave you vacation? Did you ever take vacation?

LL   Oh, a couple times. I took either a week or two weeks, but not very often. . . . One time I went to California for two weeks. And there was one time I took a week off and went down to Massachusetts to visit friends. Then sometimes it was just staying there and doing some painting on the house or whatever had to be done, you know.

SC   How come at times you just took your vacation pay and didn't take the vacation?

LL   Because I didn't feel like it, you know. When my mom got bad, I didn't really want to go very far. I set it up so if I wanted a day here and there, I'd just let them know if something happened. Like, if she went into the hospital to be operated on or something like that, they'd let me have time off.

   As a matter of fact, I got a call one time—been up all night with her. And so they let me pin-feather because I didn't want to go in and work. I hadn't had much sleep and didn't want to be working with a knife or anything like that. So I got another call to go down to the hospital because they didn't think she was going to make it—and they paid me for the time that I lost, which they usually don't. I got paid. So I mean, they treated me pretty good as far as when there was an emergency.

   The most time I missed was when I had that eye accident down there and I was out from the first of March until the last of June—but I was on workmen's comp. . . .

CC   How did that happen again? Could you explain it?

LL   I was washing down at noon time out in the New York room and the hose caught up on the leg—of course, I was pulling on it. Then when it let go, it pitched me right into the chain guard bar that went over the foot cutter—the chain that fed the feet through. I hit right up through here [points to her temple] because I had on my rain kerchief that I wore out in the sticking hole.

After that I started wearing the bumper hat—because it wasn't required for me to wear a bumper hat, you know. . . .

CC   Did you ever have long hair when you were working there?

LL   I had long hair, and I had it cut when I went out in that blood hole because it was so hard to keep up. I'd have to do it up in rollers and stuff. I just didn't want to spend the time. There was other things I had to do when I got home after putting in a long day. So I just had it cut short, because you couldn't wear it long wearing that rain kerchief—or it would stick out and be all plastered down with blood and stuff.

As a matter of fact [Linda reaches into her wallet, pulls out her high school graduation photograph and shows it to Cedric], that's how I used to wear my hair when I was in high school—right there. So it was longer. That's about the way I was wearing it when I first went down to work. . . .

[The conversation then turns to talking about Linda's ex-husband.]

CC   Is he still around the area?

LL   I see him now and then when I play at dances. . . .

SC   What do you play?

LL   Drums.

SC   I didn't know that.

LL   I play in a country band. The Golden Nuggets we go by. Last week we went up to Dixmont. This coming weekend we're playing over to Detroit [Maine]. The Snowmobile Club.

SC   Where did you learn to play drums?

LL   Well, in the fourth grade I started learning sax and reading music, right? And I was always kind of musical. But then I rented a sax . . . and had trouble with it—the pads kept falling out of it and stuff, you know, and it spent more time in the repair shop than I was playing it. So then I happened to pick up a snare drum—one snare drum—and I took one lesson on that and then went right into the school band playing the snare drum. And, of course, I could read music anyway; it just all came to me. And after a while I went back and I bought a sax and played. When they needed me on alto sax, I played that. And then I played the snare, or the bass drum, or bass sax—whatever they wanted—in the school band. Then I didn't do much after that, when I got out of high school. And then my brother had a set of drums and he kind of played around with that, but he never really pushed it, so I bought the drum set off of him. By listening to records, you know, I picked up the beat and stuff and got in with Dale Hustus and his band when he got started. And I've been with them since right after I divorced my husband, because he wouldn't let me do anything when I was married to him, as far as playing in the band. . . . Made some good money, you know. . . .

SC   What other instruments are in the group?

LL   We've got a bass player, rhythm, lead. We've got Larry, Dale, Herbie and Bill—they all play guitars.

CC   Just contemporary country, folk rock?

LL   Yup. It's country and western and old rock 'n roll. Whatever the crowd wants, we play.

SC   So what would you play in a given evening?

LL   Merle Haggard, Creedence Clearwater Revival. We've done some of Elvis Presley's songs. Usually what we start out with is a waltz, then we go to a fast one; and at the end of the evening, when people get drunk, all they want is fast ones. [laughs] Then we wind up the end of the night with a waltz. . . .

SC   How'd you get the name "Golden Nuggets"?

LL   I picked the name for the band.

CC   Do you sing?

LL   We all do. I've been playing with them since '75. We've never lost one out of the group. We stuck right together. Same people.

CC   After working at Penobscot, did you think that you'd still be looking for a job two months later?

LL   Yeah, I figured I would because jobs aren't that plentiful around here, really. And I figured it was going to take a while, especially if you went through CED with the training they were giving you. . . .

CC   Did you think there'd be the ups and downs like there has been in looking for work?

LL   Yeah, I kind of figured that. You know, you get looking around, you might get your hopes up and then the job doesn't follow through or something. And then you're going to be kind of let down, too. Something that's got to be expected when you're job hunting.

CC   What's been the most depressing thing so far?

LL   I think when I took that test at Champion. You know, I was really hoping, but that's kind of a family deal. If you don't have family in there, it's pretty hard to get in. . . . It's a good paying job and stuff, good benefits.

CC   Was going back to school different than you thought it'd be? . . .

Linda crossing her front yard. May 1988.

LL   Not much different from going to high school, but the only thing is, after twenty years, it's kind of hard to settle down again and get back into the role of studying and so forth. Then when I started taking this oil burner thing and studying eight hours a day, I just couldn't hack it with my eye. I was coming home with wicked headaches—I was in with all guys and when it came to looking at something, they would shove me right out of the way. Then I had trouble with my mom—we thought we'd have to put her in the hospital. So I just stopped taking it. And a lot of the other guys down there now, they say it's beyond them, too. The guy said right from the start, "Well, I'll show you, that's how I was taught." But he's not doing it, he's going right out of the book. Well, until you really get looking over things and have him pulling out what was in the book, it's all Greek to you. . . .

CC   When we talked before, you mentioned that if worse came to worse, you might leave the area to look for work. Has that come up yet, do you think?

LL   It hasn't really yet, because like I haven't gone to every place I can think of to put an application in yet. I want to go to Thomaston; I see in the paper that they are hiring there. I'm going to see what happens. Maybe my one eye will hold me up. I don't know.

CC   What do they do there?

LL   It's a state prison for Maine, where all the convicts go.

CC   Oh, you'd work in a state prison?

LL   Being a guard.

CC   Is it men only?

LL   No, they hire women, too.

CC   I mean, is it—the prison—

LL   For all men. The women go down around Portland somewhere. . . . They've hired other women before down there. Some of them have panned out all right. Some of them have smuggled in dope for the prisoners, so they've lost their jobs. . . .

CC   What other jobs have you applied for since you left Penobscot?

LL   Let's see, Nissen's Bakery. UPS, Robbins Brothers [Robbins Lumber Incorporated], which is a lumber mill. I had a job offer at Weaver's Bakery, but that was starting out a little nothing, $4.50 an hour, and then eventually might have worked up, but he didn't say how high it would work up. That's still open if I want to take it.

CC   That's almost equal to the unemployment you get, I bet. . . . When will you be going to Thomaston?

LL   I was hoping sometime this week. . . . It all depends on how momma is. She hasn't been very good this week. I just play it by ear. If she's fairly good during the day, then I dare to take off. If she's bad, I stick around. . . . But like I said, if I can't find anything around here, eventually I might have to go to New Hampshire or something, and get on some kind of construction that's starting up. Things are just picking up now, apparently. What I'll do when I'm down in Camden, I'll stop in at Rockland and put my name in at the state and see what they have. . . .

CC   And that's for road maintenance?

LL   Or being a flag person or something. . . . They're just starting up now, because they're doing a lot of construction on the roads and so forth.

CC   That's seasonal. It only goes through October, do you think?

LL   All depends on the weather. Sometimes they work right up almost to Christmas. . . .

CC   What will you do if you don't find work within the next three months?

LL   I'll start going out-of-state or go down to the south of Maine and see what there is to offer.

CC   Would you move down to that area?

LL   If I had to, yes, I would. Either put this place up for sale or rent it, one or the other. . . . I'd probably give it at least three months. My first extension of my unemployment doesn't run out until August. Then I can get another extension for thirteen weeks. Then probably after that I would really consider going out-of-state somewhere and trying to find something. And New Hampshire seems to be quite a place that's doing a lot of hiring, a lot of factory work and stuff like that. . . . There's everything from shoe factories to making car parts to wood.

CC   Why is there so much going on in New Hampshire and not here?

LL   I imagine the taxes have a lot to do with it.

CC   A lot more companies and corporations want to stay in a state without state tax. What do you see in the future of this area? Do you see more closings of things like Penobscot?

LL   I think eventually you'll see that around here, in Belfast, it will be developed more and possibly bring in a lot more industries. But it's going to take a while, because you've got a lot of people down in Belfast—some of whom are really pushing and other people aren't really pushing—trying to get industries there.

Linda helping a neighbor slaughter a half-dozen chickens. March 1988.

They're trying to make it a scenic place for just tourists in the summer. Well, they've tried that in Massachusetts and a lot of places like Salisbury and Newbury. They tried the scenic route the same way as Belfast—made copies of the streets from the same places like in Massachusetts. Come to find out that the tourist people just didn't bring enough money in and they had to finally start bringing in industries to help pay for the taxes and stuff. I think that's what eventually you're going to find around here.

CC   They're going to find out that they're not succeeding as a tourist area?

LL   Right. That's what mainly they're trying to do down in Belfast is make that into a tourist place. It will not work. You can't get enough tourist people coming in. And why should they hit Belfast when there's a lot prettier sights around in the state of Maine? Camden, Bar Harbor. You go down to the south of Maine, there's Old Orchard Beach, Reed State Park, and stuff like that—where there's pretty scenery and a lot of sandy beaches—more going on. That's where people are going to hit. . . .

CC   Do you think it will be quite difficult, if not impossible, to have an industry that employed four to five hundred people like Penobscot? Do you think that that will ever happen again in Belfast? Do you think it will happen within the next ten years?

LL   I don't know about the next ten years. There's been a lot of business people coming in and looking things over. And if you've been reading the *Republican Journal* and the *Independent*, and the way they fight and bicker down there in Belfast about wanting an industry in and not wanting one in and so forth—and what it's going to do to the land and the water and so forth—I'd like to see it myself. . . . I'd like to see more industries in and around. It helps on your taxes, and it keeps the store owners happy. You know, people earning money are going to spend it. But if you've got tourist people coming in only during the summer—and you're never going to get that much as far as I'm concerned, in Belfast, because there's nothing really that scenic. You've only got what?—maybe three to four months that tourists are going to come in and that's going to be it. To me, Belfast is better off having something year-round.

CC   Something solid.

LL   Solid, that people can earn money.

CC   In the meantime, what will people like yourself be doing? Do you think they'll be moving out of the area?

LL   The young people like me will be moving where there's jobs. I've seen it the last ten years. You know, you hardly see a young couple stay here that's been brought up. They go elsewhere in the big cities where there's money. Or go out of state where there's money and then eventually, when they get older, they come back and they retire and buy a place around here.

See, way back, there used to be a lot of things right around here in Brooks. There was a canning factory. There was Maine Reduction up there [Maine Reduction Company, Inc., a fertilizer business]. We used to have a bank way back and a drugstore, and that's all gone. . . . I'm talking about Brooks alone, to say nothing about Belfast—what's going out of Belfast. Belfast has lost a lot of industries in, I would say, the past five to eight years. For one thing, the foreign markets are cheaper. I mean, as far as importing stuff, it's a lot cheaper than what we can do it here. . . .

CC I recently saw a cover to a magazine—I guess it was December of 1986, which would make it a year and a half old now—but the cover of it said, "Has the Maine work ethic died?" How do you feel about that? Do you think it's changing?

LL I think, yeah, it's dying, because a lot of industries don't want to move up this way, on account of it costs so much for electricity, fuel, or shipping things back and forth. And besides that, down South, the labor is cheaper than it is up here.

CC So you think over the last twenty years, that the industries who are deciding to go somewhere, they're not choosing Maine, they're choosing southern states over Maine. So do you think that people here in Maine will realize that and try and—

LL I think they've realized it some now, because I know there's been a couple of industries that they wanted into Belfast and they had checked into it. And the people just didn't want to move into Belfast because it cost so much. They went down to the south of Maine or some place where it was a little bit cheaper, as far as the freight, the electricity, and taxes and so forth. See, you take more industries that are around, okay, the cheaper everybody's taxes are going to be on the whole. But if you take one outfit that moved up here in Belfast, he's going to be taxed outrageous because he's the only industry going. And that's how they figure it. But the more industries around, the cheaper your taxes are. Because all these industries are chipping in, too. . . .

CC Twenty years working at Penobscot, what do you think you learned in those twenty years as far as being a working-class woman?

LL Can't say I learned too much from just the type of job I did. Well, you get looking at it and you want to try to find something with a little bit better pay, something with a little cleaner environment, just to try to better yourself. Something that would be year-round, not just part-time. I'm getting bored. You know, if I can find something that I can at least get into that's steady and build up to a good seniority, okay? Getting a pension, and fairly good pay so you'd maybe be able to save something, not scraping by like I was at Penobscot.

CC So working at Penobscot you pretty much lived from hand to mouth and month to month?

LL Just about week to week.

CC Well, do you have any further comments, anything you wanted to add?

LL Only time will tell, I guess—and just keep job hunting. I look at the *Republican Journal* and the *Independent*, each week that comes out. And I have the *Bangor Daily [News]* coming every day, and I look through the Waterville paper. I've got friends over in Unity that have the Waterville paper, too, and they're keeping an eye out on something they think that I might like to do. It's just going to take a matter of time, I guess. . . . As far as money coming in.

Serving food at a Brooks Volunteer Fire Department supper. April 1988.

You know, I want to wait until I can at least get maybe seven, eight—maybe ten dollars an hour. It's going to take a while.

CC   What would be the lowest you would take?

LL   Probably just about what I was making at the plant, which was $5.69. I wouldn't go anything lower than that. . . . Bob [Linda's friend who owns Gallagher's Galley] was talking with some people today—one that came up from Florida—I guess he was applying for a job up to UPS. He said that most places down there in Florida were only paying five dollars an hour. They claim there's all kinds of jobs, but they don't want to pay anybody anything, either. And how the heck do people live on five dollars an hour down in Florida where the cost of living is—

CC   Yeah. What do you think are some of the advantages of living here in Maine?

LL   Okay, you've got the four seasons. You know, you've got your spring, you got your summer, you got your fall, you got winter. The climate here, I mean, we don't have any tornadoes. Hurricanes once in a great while, but it's nothing really serious. We don't have any poison bugs or snakes. And usually you have enough decent land so you can grow a garden or something and try to get by. Try to help on the cost of living. . . . And then you've got cleaner air, and yet that's getting bad with this acid rain and so forth from the plants—which isn't from the state of Maine—it's coming across. There's a lot of things you can do in the state of Maine. It's a pretty state. You can hunt, you can fish, you can go sightseeing. There's a lot of pretty scenery around.

CC   You do hunt and fish yourself, don't you?

LL   Yes, I do.

CC   And that would be a good reason for you to stay? I'm sure you could hunt and fish elsewhere.

Learning computer skills at the Coastal Economic Development office in Belfast, Maine. June 1988.

LL   Yeah, but of course you know the surroundings, too, and that helps. . . . And I don't really care for the big city life, either. But if I have to do it, I've got to do it. I'll keep looking around—I want to hit the job service in Waterville and I'll probably go to Bangor and see what they have to offer, too. . . .

CC   After Mr. Lewis died, were you looking for work that summer?

LL   No, I didn't really. At that time I figured I'd better stay if the place closed, try to get my severance pay and what I could out of the company. No, I didn't really look.

CC   So, in other words, when you were there, realizing that it might close, if you'd have quit, you wouldn't have gotten your severance pay.

LL   No, I would have lost everything.

CC   Even though you recently got your severance, it's not as much as you thought it should have been.

LL   It's better than nothing. Some of the poor guys there at the grain mill and the hatchery, they didn't get it, because it was under sixty-seven people. See, there's a clause in the thing on severance pay that you've got to have—at least employ—a hundred people.

CC   Which Penobscot certainly did.

LL   Penobscot had over a hundred people. Small branches went by Bayside Enterprises. Even though the guys at the grain mill, truck drivers, went along with our contract . . . and they were in the union, they [Bayside Enterprises, Inc.] were off in a different branch and they didn't employ over a hundred people.

CC   Bayside is not owned by Penobscot?

LL   Yes, it is. But it's a branch off of Penobscot itself. . . . Penobscot owns a hatchery which went by Bayside. Penobscot owned the grain mills.

Playing drums with the Golden Nuggets at a campground in Dixmont, Maine. June 1988.

CC   Which is run by Bayside.

LL   Which is run by Penobscot but went by Bayside.

CC   So even though they owned Bayside, they couldn't give those men and women severance pay. Did they try and fight that?

LL   I don't know if they're gonna try and fight it or not. I doubt it. By the time you got a lawyer, and you tried fighting it and had hearings and stuff, the lawyer would wind up with most of the money. Because I think Fort Halifax hired a lawyer so they could get their money. And by the time they did get anything, the lawyers had eaten it up with their fees.

CC   Yeah. Have you talked to friends that you used to work with at Penobscot recently? Has anyone had a good success story that you know of—that's gotten a better job?

LL   No. There's that Jenny Whitaker. She's not happy there at that shoe place there in Belfast. She says they treat you worse than they did at Penobscot. A lot of them are out at Fort Halifax, and they love it out there.

      [The telephone rings: a friend from Florida phoning to tell Linda about a job possibility in Florida. She and Cedric discuss the prospect of Linda living in Florida and then pick up where they left off.]

LL   Just a few have gone on to Fort Halifax—a couple of them are working down there at that fish place in Rockland. Of course, Jenny went to that shoe place there in Belfast; some have gone down to the frozen food locker, but there's not many.

CC   Do you know of any that have moved out-of-state—left?

LL   Not really, because I haven't been in touch with everybody. I know one woman just as soon as the plant was closing, she was going back and marrying a guy down in Massachusetts. That's only one that I know of. The rest of them, I don't know what's happened to them.

CC   Well, I really can't think of anything else. I just kind of wanted to get your feelings of what it's been like to be unemployed for the first time in twenty years.

LL   Hard. [laughs] Frustrating, really, because I've got to start finding something that I can hopefully work in. Something that I will enjoy for the rest of my life and build up my seniority again, my pension plan, you know. Then you wind up [asking yourself]—are you going to be able to find a job by the time your unemployment runs out? So those are the main things you've got to worry about.

CC   Have you noticed a change in your personal life? I mean, do you sleep differently, or do you—

LL   Yeah. I stay up late now. Maybe if I feel like it, I sleep in the morning—there's no set schedule, you know. If I have something to do, I'll set the alarm and I'll get up. If there isn't, I'll just lay in bed or stay up half the night watching programs that I never did watch before because I was too tired and would fall asleep if I did.

CC   Well, what if Nissen called you tomorrow and wanted you to go to work, would you go to work for them right away or—

LL   Right away. I wouldn't hesitate.

CC   And the same if Sysco called, you'd—

LL   Right, I'd start right in for them. . . .

CC   Have you looked into the possibility of getting a license to drive bigger trucks?

LL   That course is starting right up, but they're still having a problem trying to find out about—where I've got that one eye.

CC   Do they really harp you on that?

LL   This one eye, I mean, some people with one eye, it affects them as far as distance and judgment and so forth, but it doesn't me.

CC   After you lost it, was there a readjustment period? . . .

LL   I had to learn to walk again—balance, a lot of things. It did affect me at the first. But, you know, you get used to it. Nature compensates for the loss of an eye or something. It takes over.

CC   Do you know of anyone else at Penobscot that was injured in that way?

LL   As far as an eye? Ahh—yes, but of course, he lost his eye entirely, had to have it removed. I don't know what kind of settlement he got or anything like that. There's been people that hurt their back and they got a good settlement out of that, but I don't know how much. . . . They had a way that if—you know, a loss of a finger was so much, and a loss of a hand was so much, or an arm was so much, or an eye was so much, and that's how they went. But I don't think they really realize just what one eye—how it limits you in a lot of things. And it hurts you for good jobs, too. But if I have to, I can reopen this court case if it interferes with a lot of jobs, and there's proof of it.

CC   You mean, you can—

LL   Go back and try to get another settlement.

CC   What do you miss most about Penobscot, if you were to pick something?

LL   What do I miss most? Some of the people I worked with. . . .

CC   Did you have much of a social life with them outside of—

LL   No, I didn't. . . . Penobscot wasn't much of a hand to have anything going for the working people, any kind of leagues or anything like that, you know, bowling or playing softball or anything like that. We couldn't get a Christmas party or anything out of them, except for what we'd get together ourselves. . . .

CC   If that's what you miss most, what about Penobscot do you least miss? . . .

LL   The hassle. Counting every minute of your time. You know, you had to keep busy every minute of your time. I mean, if you slacked off in your work, then the production would be bad. Now that part I don't miss at all. You had to do a good job in order to keep your job, or you were out the door.

CC   Did they follow you around and watch you work? . . .

LL   Sure. They watched the birds to see how they were bled out and if you were doing your job. Or they would try some dirty deal to see what they could get away with. . . . Like wash down and stuff like that, try to take your time away, or cheat you out of it. Just give you a hassle, you know. But they didn't get away with much with me. Because when I figured that I was in the right, I went all the way. [laughs] I even threatened to get OSHA [Occupational

Safety and Health Administration] in there if they didn't meet me halfway. I don't know how many times I threatened to get OSHA in there and close that place down, if they didn't get some of the things to make my job easier—or just get off my back. That hanging area wasn't safe, the sticking room—the environment being cold in the winter and hot in the summer. You know, it states right in that contract that under bad conditions, we didn't have to work—or unsafe conditions. You know, the dust and stuff. Once you had one part closed down, the plant wouldn't have been able to operate.

CC   That's true. Was the dust bad in the room that you were in?

LL   Yes, it was. . . . In the summer it was wicked. And I didn't have that big sucking fan like the other side [Line Two] had, either. See, if they'd had sucking fans going up through the roof, it would have been better.

CC   Who else was on your side as far as the workers—were there other workers that threatened to get OSHA in there?

LL   A few did, the smart ones. The others didn't even bother to try to stand up for themselves. You had to do it for them. . . . Not unless they came and they complained or wanted to file a grievance. Then you'd try putting the pressure to whoever was plant manager.

CC   Was there quite a turnover rate there at Penobscot? . . .

LL   Yeah. Especially more so out in the hanging area. You know, they'd come in maybe a week or two if they were able to keep up with the line and do the job. Then they had to wait like six months before they could get top pay. Well, no one was going to stay out there and take that dust and the ammonia and so forth and wait that long to get top pay. They'd just walk right out the door.

Linda checking the employment board at the Coastal Economic Development office. August 1988.

CC   So maybe you could tell me what it's been like to be unemployed since you left Penobscot. It's been, what, almost six months? . . . When you were laid off at Penobscot, did you think that you'd be unemployed this long?

LL   I figured, you know, in a short time I would find a job. But what hurt, too, was that a lot of people hired school kids to get by for the summer, see—cheaper help. Now that school kids are back things are just starting to pick up. . . .

CC   Tell me about the job that you do now. When you started working, did you think that it would be something that you'd want to stay at? Were you glad to hear about it, or is just another—

LL   It was just another job, and I was glad that it came along because my unemployment was running out.

CC   So if it hadn't come along and your unemployment would've run out, would you have gotten another extension?

LL   I would've had to go down for a hearing, and then I would've been getting something from Augusta . . . to get you through until you did find a job.

CC   Tell me a little bit about the duties of what you do there at Crowe Rope.

First week on the job at Belfast Rope, Belfast, Maine. September 1988.

LL Just mainly they're showing you how to run the machines there and what to do. This last machine I'm on now you have twelve spools of fine nylon stuff that's twisted, and it makes ¼ inch rope. And you've got a gauge thing and when it hits fifteen-hundred, then it kicks off. And then you have to cut the rope, put tape around it and put it on another spool and reset it—and so forth, like that. And all those twelve spools, if they start getting empty, then you have to heat it and splice in and start the machine up again.

CC Tell me about how you can make more money doing piece work.

LL Well, just by keeping the machine running, like getting eight hours out of it and getting a number of spools off of it in that eight hours. They weigh it.

CC So they have a certain number of spools and if you get above and beyond that, then you make *x* amount?

LL Yup, they put you on piece work.

CC So how long does it take to get to that point?

LL Well, it all depends. Like if you get full spools, you should be able to run all right without any problems, you know—if the machinery doesn't break down, too. So it's just a matter of learning, I guess, about five or six weeks [the training period].

CC Is there a chance for promotion? Or is there any place you can go in the company, like to a supervisor?

LL Not unless you learn all the machinery and want to be a foreman or something. . . . Well, you'd have to know a lot about the machinery and stuff. Probably in time, yeah, it's something you could learn.

CC So what was the interview like when you went down there?

LL Oh, they just told you what the benefits were, that you didn't have any breaks or stuff like that—where you were watching the machinery half the time, just sitting there. You'd have to eat your meal right there, a piece of paper you had to sign for that. And all your benefits and profit sharing and your insurance and life insurance, and about being there on time. For three months, you'll get a hundred dollar quota or something—if you're there. And that's just about it.

CC Do they give you any lunch break time?

LL Nope, you eat right there running the machine.

CC Because the machines can't stop?

LL Right. . . . But a lot of times you're just sitting there, so you've got a chance to grab something to eat, you know.

CC You've only been there a short while, but how does it compare to working at Penobscot?

LL A lot cleaner. Pays a little bit better. Even $5.50—you'll be bringing home clear, $181 [per week]. Down there at Penobscot, you never knew what you were going to be bringing home. You never knew what hours you were to get, either.

CC How come?

LL Because it varied on the order for birds they had. . . . You could maybe work like five hours, maybe six hours, six and a half, seven. You know, you never knew from one day to the next. I've worked ten hours before. That's when we were doing a lot of big birds—capons and roasters together. . . .

CC   So at Crowe Rope would you ever be in the position to get overtime?

LL   Oh, yeah, you could get in some overtime. If the chance came along on certain machinery—if they needed to get out more rope—yeah, I probably would do it.

CC   How else does it compare to working at Penobscot besides it being cleaner?

LL   You're working by yourself. You're not around a bunch of people that might cause trouble for you on the line. . . . Everybody's watching their own machines, standing there, and that's it. You don't have that much time to talk with anybody, you know. . . .

CC   Have you seen or talked to anybody that you used to work with at Penobscot?

LL   A few people.

CC   What have they said about their condition?

LL   Some are not happy with the jobs they've got. Others are happy. . . . The only reason I tried this Belfast Rope company was it was close to home, you know. And I've traveled that road, so I knew what I'd be getting into come winter and stuff—and there's not much wear and tear on your car. Benefits were good.

CC   Do you feel pretty fortunate in having a job?

LL   Yeah, I do.

CC   Did you celebrate when you heard about it?

LL   [Laughs] Bob took me out for supper [Linda's friend who owns Gallagher's Galley].

CC   It's been almost a year since you left Penobscot. Do you feel like you're any better off now than you were a year ago?

LL   The only way I can figure I'm better off is making more money per hour.

CC   How about the job situation? How much different is it?

LL   A lot cleaner job. It seems that the company that I'm working for now is more eager to please the worker and there's no union involved.

CC   There's no union?

LL   No union at all. We had a meeting not too long ago. They wanted to try to see the place run a little bit better. And they're willing to take suggestions from the workers and try to make it easier for everybody.

CC   Do you think that's better, not having a union? I mean, compare not having a union as to having a union that you had at Penobscot. Do you think you're better off without union benefits?

LL   If you've got good people to work for, I think you're better off without a union. Because eventually—and I've seen it on television and in other states—a lot of the unions put a lot of the small places right out of business by upping your wages so the company just couldn't afford to pay the people.

Linda working at Belfast Rope.

. . . But if they're bad people to work for, then I suggest people go out and try to get a union in and try to straighten out the mess—if you can't work with the people. . . .

CC   And the place that you're working now is Belfast Rope? Was it ever called Crowe Rope?

LL   It goes by Crowe Rope, but all the different branches around go by different names. [Belfast Rope was a division of Crowe Rope Industries.] I guess it's more or less to try to help keep the union out. See, if they knew it was one great big outfit and stuff—there's more to it, but I really don't understand why. But each place is working for the main office there at Warren [Maine], which is Crowe Rope. But Belfast goes by Belfast Rope, and I don't know what Unity goes by. And they've got two in Morrill. They're starting one up in Prospect, they're starting one up in Thorndike, and, of course, the main office in Warren. I think there's another one out in Liberty.

CC   Is the one in Belfast, is it about the same size as the other rope companies in those other towns, or do you know that?

LL   Yeah, about the same size. Of course, I haven't been inside the chicken houses they've converted over.

CC   They're converting chicken houses into—

LL   They [Crowe Rope] have bought a lot of chicken houses that they're converting over. The one in Prospect is a chicken house, the one in Thorndike is a chicken house. . . . One that I've seen on—I think it's [Route] 220 going down into Liberty, heading towards Washington—that was a chicken house converted over.

CC   So even though the poultry business is no longer in the area, the aftermath—meaning chicken barns, etcetera—can be used to an advantage of other industries. You know, a lot of people thought that they'd be raising rabbits or mushrooms, something agricultural.

LL   Or tearing down the chicken houses.

CC   But they're using them as rope factories—that's very interesting. . . . I've asked this in one way or another, but how much different is your new job? I mean, different in the sense of labor that you actually put forth, I mean, physical labor or challenge. Are you more challenged mentally? . . .

LL   You used your arms more at Penobscot, because you were busy all the time swinging your arms. At the job I have now, you have to lift a few things, but they're not that heavy, and the things that are really heavy now, they've got hoisters up to five hundred pounds who do the heavy work. So I would say I'm not working half as hard as I did at Penobscot. . . . As far as challenge, the job that I'm on now is piece-rate, so you're trying to put out as much as you can, you know, in an eight-hour day.

CC   So it's all up to you how much work you get done?

LL   Providing I have the stock. . . .

CC   You know, the last time we talked we figured on the average day you twine about ten miles of rope. Compare that to Penobscot when you were seeing eighty to a hundred thousand chickens a day. How do you feel about that comparison? Looking at ten miles of rope as opposed to looking at all those chickens.

LL   Well, I tell you, looking at ten miles of rope goes a lot faster than watching chickens go by on a line. You'd get hypnotized watching the chickens, but there's so many things that you're looking at all the time on these three different machines. You know, it isn't like looking at one steady line going right around. Time goes fast working at Belfast Rope. . . .

CC   A few minutes ago you gave me about a dozen names of people you knew by name, that you could recall quickly that you worked with. Have any of them had to leave the area that you know of?

LL   No, they've all—the ones that I put down on that paper have all found jobs.

CC   Did any of them take as long as you did to find a job?

LL   There are still some people I know now that's not on that list that haven't found a job. They're waiting.

CC   Are they still getting unemployment benefits, do you think?

LL   Still getting some kind of schooling. I guess from what I understand, it's about ready to run out.

CC   When you heard about Penobscot closing, did you think it was really going to devastate the community? . . .

LL   I figured we would have a tough time because there's not that many industries right there in Belfast to take over the people getting out of Penobscot. But Frozen Food has hired quite a lot, and that Etonic shoe place [Etonic Tretorn Incorporated], that's hired quite a few. There's quite a few that were hired by the rope company. The shirt place down there, the tee-shirts, you know. And some have traveled to Camden, some have gone on construction. One is working over to Unity College as a janitor. Some are working as janitors in schools. Some are driving trucks for oil rigs that are working on furnaces and stuff.

CC   So the people that you mentioned here . . . were they what you could call old-timers at Penobscot? In other words, were they there for longer than five or ten years?

LL   Quite a lot of them were, yup.

CC   So they really tried to stay in the area. I mean, they had more roots than, say, some of the folks who'd only been at Penobscot for only a few months or a year. Do you think a lot of those people left the area?

LL   Some of the young people did. Some of them went right out of state— Massachusetts, Connecticut.

CC   Yeah. Do you feel that the community—in other words, Waldo County in general—is better off without Penobscot?

LL   I think a lot of people and places, including businesses, were hurt when Penobscot closed. It'll take a while for things to get back the way they were when Penobscot was running—people finding jobs and getting back on their feet.

CC   So do you think that there will be stability in Belfast with just the small amount of industry that it has, like the shoe place that—

LL   I think you've got to have more than what's right in Belfast right now. More business starting up or industries. . . . Well, you see, that shoe place just started up again that used to be Waldo Shoe [Corporation]. And to me I'd be kind of shaky about that, because Korea and Japan are sending over a lot of stuff that's a lot cheaper than what we can put right out here.

And that's another thing, too, that's hurt us is the American people have put up a lot of places over there in Japan, Korea, and so forth, making cars, making shoes, and then ship it back here and sell it a lot cheaper than making stuff right here in the United States. . . . I think way back they should have been looking out more for the American people—try to keep business right here. . . .

CC   How do you feel as far as Belfast Rope? Do you feel pretty secure there?

LL   Yes. They've been around for a long time in different places. And they're just expanding more around here.

CC   Do you get the feeling that it's a more stable environment there [than at Penobscot]?

LL   I've seen a lot of people go in and out at Belfast Rope, but it all depends on how bad you want to work. You know, it was the same way at Penobscot. If you didn't want to work, you saw people go in and out of the door. And I seen quite a few at Belfast Rope. . . .

CC   So how much an hour are you paid now?

LL   I average between $6.50 to $6.75 to $6.80.

CC $5.50 is the base pay and then anything—

LL   Up above that is [piece rate].

CC   And you think that that's a real competitive wage in this area?

LL   Darn good. Most of what they're getting elsewhere, like at the sardine place or Frozen Food. . . . A lot of them are averaging maybe $5.50, $5.75, to $6.00. Of course, at the sardine place, if you get all piece-rate down there you can make darn good money. But then they're laid off quite a lot, too, when they don't have the fish coming in and so forth.

CC   Do you think that they would some day close, just like Penobscot did?

LL   No. The sardine place has been there ever since I can remember. . . .

CC   Do you think that you're better off than most of the people that walked away a year ago?

LL   I would say so, yeah. . . . At the time that Penobscot closed, there was so many people that it was just luck if you got into a good paying job. You know, you were talking over, what, five to eight hundred people. It was at least five hundred people at Penobscot alone, and that wasn't including the grain mill, the hatchery, and the growers. . . .

CC   Are you glad that you stayed in Maine? Do you think that you would have been better off having gone to Boston or Portsmouth?

LL   I probably could have made more money going out-of-state. But I'm around here and kind of help out with my folks.

CC   Plus you'll be able to play with the band. . . .

LL   Right. Play with the band. Be with the fire department.

CC   Go hunting.

LL   Go hunting, go fishing.

CC   Be a true Mainer.

LL   Yeah. . . . Just doesn't seem possible that it's been almost a year now since the place closed. Time goes fast. About this time last year, I was worrying what was going to happen after it closed, and how long I'd be trying to find a job and get back on my feet.

[The tape begins with Cedric and Linda discussing the fact that Linda was one of the few women who worked in the blood tunnel. As Cedric's closing interview with Linda, much of this interview reflects back to her experience at Penobscot, focusing on her role as a woman in the plant.]

CC   Why didn't you consider white-collar employment when you first started, right out of high school, such as a bank teller or secretary?

LL   They didn't pay anything—minimum wage. Who can live on minimum wage if you're a single person? You know, you go where the money is. At the time, way back when I started at Penobscot, you could bring home a good pay check and were able to save. . . .

CC   Just estimate, what was the ratio of men to women at Penobscot? How many women do you think worked there, like a percentage, and how many men?

LL   Oh, I think it depends. Sometimes there might have been more women than men. Let's say 60 percent women and 40 percent men—and then it might even out, you know, 50-50. But that's just what you're figuring in the plant. You've got to figure all the farms, the hatchery, the grain mill—there were quite a lot of men there at the hatchery. I guess there was all men there at the grain mill, except for one woman they had working the office. But down at the plant, you know, it varied.

CC   Were the jobs different—I mean, did women do different jobs than men, for the most part?

LL   The only thing that I think the men did different from women was hanging, which I had done when they were in a pinch.

CC   Do you mean outside, off of the trucks?

LL   Yeah, out where the unloading dock—. And I don't think they ever had a woman truck driver. Just recently, before the plant closed, they had some on the pickup crew that drove trucks, and she did more damage than she did good. I can't ever recall any forklift drivers down there as women. And as far as loading the frozen stuff, that was all done by men. It was mainly right there in the plant that the men and women had the same jobs, you know, on the eviscerating line, the cut-up line.

CC   Do you feel that you were much different from some of the other women in the fact that you were single and supporting yourself? Or were there other women that you knew that were doing that?

LL   Yeah, there were a lot of women that were single and working in there, or they had kids to raise.

CC   Did you feel any sort of bond with them at all?

LL   No. I didn't associate with many. Well, I didn't have a chance on account of I couldn't go through the plant the way I came out of that sticking hole, the way I was looking—all covered with blood, dust, and stuff. I could not walk out with the birds being open, or the inspectors would have closed the line right down. You know, I had to stay out in my part, so the only time that I actually had any chance of going upstairs was at noon-time, and then it was a half an hour break that we had. And it was tough trying to get off that stuff, get cleaned up, and go up. . . .

CC   What, according to you, should be the company's responsibilities to its worker?

LL   Hmm. Responsibility? They provided us with a job, I mean they—oh, I think in some cases they could have paid a little bit better. But Penobscot was there for a long time. It helped the towns around, you know, with the people working and bringing money back into those towns. It helped Belfast out. I think in some cases we could have had better insurance and stuff, but the insurance we had was all right. It got worse as time went on, but a lot of the places have had to either make people pay for their own insurance—or pay for part of it . . .

CC   Did you feel any kind of allegiance to Penobscot or any kind of loyalty?

LL   Well, not really. I mean, when I went in there I did my job, you know. I was getting paid to do a job and do it right. I was never one, ever since I was a teenager, to shirk off on a job, you know. I did it, I did it well—or not bother to do it at all, if you're not going to do a good job. But, of course, that sticking job, you had to be on the ball, or you could cost the company a lot of money. Because once those birds didn't bleed out, they had to be thrown down into the rendering. So if you didn't do your job, they would have got you out of there.

CC   So your job in the sticking hole was quite important?

LL   And very demanding—I mean, you had to be right on the ball. . . .

CC   Okay. What do you think of the word *feminism*?

LL   What do I think of it? The way I look at it, it doesn't make a difference if it's a man or a woman, if they're qualified to do the job—fine. I don't believe in a man getting more pay than a woman doing the same job. I figure if a man or a woman do the job, they should get paid the same. But a lot of this other stuff, you know, that women try to go for, some of it I was against.

CC   Which?

LL   Oh, I can't remember now some of the things that were brought up in the past about that. But as far as a paying job, I think the man and a woman, if they're doing the same type of job, they should get paid the same. But as far as a woman trying to go out and prove that she's better than a man, you know, I don't go for that. But as far as people working right beside each other doing the same kind of work—

CC   Do you feel you were treated fairly as a woman in the plant?

LL   Yeah. I mean, usually if anything went wrong, I would go and talk with them and they'd try to correct the problem. There were a few times, you know, you had to haul in a foreman . . . but usually, after a while, they would look into the problem and take care of it. I wouldn't let anybody walk over me, no. If I figured I was right, I'd stand my ground—whether they liked it or they didn't.

CC   Do you think that women face more problems on the job and off the job than what men do?

LL   No. Well, of course, women had housework, but some of the men, too, would help, you know, if they were married.

CC   There were married couples working there?

LL   Yeah, some were good people, they would pitch in and help out, too, at home. But then some—male chauvinists anyway—they figured, well, they been out at work they don't need to do anything at home or try to take a load off from the wife that was out working. But nowadays you see more men help out the wives that are out working, too, so they can both make ends meet. You know, they can do some housework or maybe do the dishes or laundry or something or shopping—more than what they used to way back. . . .

CC   Okay, about your job . . . about working in the sticking hole.

LL   The sticking hole—a lot of men wouldn't do the job that I was doing. Either the blood bothered them or the dust bothered them. Of course, they had quite a lot of men stickers but, still, there were a lot of men that tried it but never could hack it. Some just didn't want to sit down, it was boring to them.

CC   You mentioned that you thought that you were the first woman in the industry to have the job in the sticking hole. Could you tell me a little bit about that?

LL   Just what information I could gather, that no woman was really interested in going in killing anywhere around—as far as the state of Maine. I don't know about in other states, but I guess I was the only one that stuck it out killing birds and stuff.

CC   Do you think you were the longest standing sticker at Penobscot?

LL   No, they had some other people that had been sticking for quite a long time that finally they either went down to rendering or, you know, took a foreman's job. . . .

CC   I wondered. Who would take your place on vacations?

LL   At the end of it, it was pretty hard, but they had one woman after me—it was Alex there—she was a spare sticker. They had a few spare stickers that would fill in, but at the end it got so you couldn't even find a spare sticker to go in there. . . . Some people couldn't hack the blood or it bothered their shoulder or they'd have tendinitis in the shoulder.

[At this point, Cedric and Linda begin to discuss the knives she used and then stops the interview shortly afterward. Linda then begins to talk about working with poultry with her father when she was a child. Cedric turns on the tape recorder and catches her in midsentence.]

LL   —Taking blood samples. And when I was there at the hatchery, before they transferred me down there at the plant, I used to de-beak them, inject them, defeather them, sex them. So I mean, right up through, I've just been right around birds all the time.

Linda looking into a machine at Belfast Rope.

CC So you've known chickens all your life?

LL Right.

CC And have worked with them since a child.

LL Yup. From laying hens to you name it. . . . Of course, when my father had laying hens, I used to go in and feed them, gather eggs. And, of course, back then we had what we called brooder stoves and stuff that we'd put coal in to keep the chicken house warm. You had waterers that you had to clean out and fill up and—nothing was automatic back then, you know. Everything had to be done by hand. If there was a flood, you had to clean out the wet litter and put in dry or there'd be a lot of ammonia and the birds would get burned from the ammonia. And I used to go in and feed up chickens for other people. And when they had baby chicks come in, I'd clean out the litter, spread new shavings, and sweep down and stuff, and wash the waterers, and lay out paper to feed the baby chicks on.

Then as I got older, I went working with my father there. What I mainly did was you had a box with a hundred bottles and you had bands, and when my father would prick the vein under the wing there to draw a little blood, I had to take that bottle and it had to coincide with the number on the band, you know. So when he took it to the University of Maine—if they found out a certain bird was running a kind of disease that could spread to the rest of the flock—then they'd go back in and either put some kind of vaccine in the water or inject them or something so they wouldn't be sick. So I did that.

And I used to catch and de-toe them and stuff, whatever had to be done, you know, when we were there doing the birds. . . .

CC   What did your dad feel like when Penobscot closed? Did he talk much about that? Did he have any comments when he saw the industry failing here in Maine?

LL   He kind of surmised that—with the way it was costing to ship grain up and electricity, fuel, and they were always pushing the farmers into newer equipment and stuff, instead of getting by with what they had—that sooner or later he kind of figured it would go downhill. That the southern markets with cheaper labor would take over the industry as far as chicken. And that's just what happened. The southern states have got it. They opened up Fort Halifax over there for a while. That's closed down now. I don't know the reason why. But, no, chicken is out of here in the state of Maine.

*[The following taped conversation took place five years after Cedric's last
interview. The goal was to clarify points Linda had made in earlier interviews
and to address several assumptions we had made. At the start of the conversation,
Linda and I discuss her reasons for taking the job at Penobscot, her work on the
family farm as a child, and her current role in community activities.]*

AR   Well, how do you feel about Crowe Rope now? How's your work going there?

LL   Hmph. They almost filed bankruptcy. I thought I was going to be without a
job, but they borrowed the money to keep going, hoping they can get out of
the situation they're in. Of course, we had another fire. That hurt. And then
they ordered a million dollar computer, and that didn't work out. So we've
taken a cut in our pay check, 7 percent. . . .

AR   So what do you think they could do that would improve [the situation]?

LL   Ooh. For one, I would cut down a lot of the high-paying jobs. Of course,
you've got to have certain people to do office work and do inventory work and
so forth. You've got engineers. But I think some of it could be eliminated and
cut down. And I think they could order cheap stuff to get by, you know, as far
as yarn and stuff. And sometimes it doesn't run very good. You get poor
quality and stuff. I think if they got a little bit better stuff, things would run a
lot better. Of course, it'd be more costly, too.

AR   Hmm. How do you feel about your work, knowing that?

LL   Well, I do the best I can and, you know, that's the company's fault. . . .

AR   What's the makeup of the folks who work there? How many men? How
many women?

LL   More men than there are women.

AR   What kind of jobs are they doing, the men and the women?

LL   Well, big rope, extruder. Because those extruder bobbins, when you get your
poly-pro on that, you've gotten over a hundred pounds that you've got to lift.
So there's a lot of lifting involved.

AR   Who does those jobs?

LL   Men.

AR   Yeah. What about the women?

LL   There's only one at Belfast [meaning Crowe Rope in Belfast]. That's me,
besides the office help.

AR   Wow. So you're the only woman on the floor? Why do you suppose that is?

LL   I don't know. Never figured it out, whether they wanted to cover their butts
having at least one woman, you know, in the plant. I don't know. . . .

AR   What about with your job here? Do you take more or less pride, or whatever,

Linda and her father, Phillip Lord, in their garden, Brooks, Maine. Summer 1992.

in comparison to working in the blood tunnel?

LL   I try to do the best I can. I'm one that I won't *half* do anything. I try to make the best type of rope I can. I try to keep my area picked up, you know, looking nice, keep my machines clean.

AR   And where did you learn all of that? Where did you learn to be so conscientious about your work? . . .

LL   It stems from my father drilling it into me. Well, of course, when we were going to school, he tried to tell us to do well and not to go back and have to do things over. And it was the same way around here as far as doing chores and stuff. And it just more or less stuck with me in growing up.

[We talk about her father and mother, who have both passed away.]

AR   So how are things now? How's life compared to when you were at Penobscot? It's been six years, right?

LL   Well, the economy is tight around here. And OSHA is just making it kind of hard for the companies that are still going. There are rules and regulations of what you have to wear and what you can't wear. And, of course, you know, people have been buying steel-toe shoes at Ames [Department Store] now. And if they don't meet a certain number that's put on that, then they can fine

Downtown Belfast, Maine. Summer 1994.

the company. They're just making it rough on everybody. It's even that way in the fire department.

AR   What's their reason for the regulations?

LL   Oh, I think they're trying to squeeze the small people out. Just have big businesses. That's what it amounts to.

AR   What about—? But I thought their role was to protect the worker for safety?

LL   Oh, my God! You stop to think—like in the [Brooks Volunteer] Fire Department—if people outside fought fires and stuff, we didn't have half the gear that we have now, and you didn't have any casualties or bad lungs or anything like that.

AR   So you don't think it's worth all that?

LL   No. I think you've got a lot of big bugs that are sitting on their ass, drawing over probably $150,000 a year, making it hard for the working people. And the companies are trying to keep going. . . . I don't know. A lot of people are getting awful fed up now and starting to fight back. Getting up petitions and fighting them, you know, through the legislature and Augusta. Whatever area it's in—the working people are getting fed up. They're being taxed to death and insured to death and, you know, it just can't keep going this way. . . .

AR   Do you remember Carolyn [Chute]'s remarks at the opening event? She talks a lot about work and the Maine work ethic. . . . She thinks the Maine work ethic is overrated. Why should that be such a great thing, to work, to do backbreaking work, basically?

LL   Well, sometimes you've got to do it, you know, in order to survive.

AR   Yeah. I mean, she's done it. It's not like she hasn't done it. But I think she feels like our culture judges people a lot for that. How do you—

LL   Well, I think people always judge Maine people hard. They think we're a bunch of hicks that are still back in the old times, with no running water and outhouses. But it's more or less a lot of country stuff. You've got to work in order to live. And you've got to work darn hard. . . .

AR   Well, what about the future with Crowe Rope? Do you think you're going to try and hang in there? Or do you see other options in the area?

LL   Well, I'm going back down to Thomaston [State Prison] again and try that and see what happens. Because sooner or later my age is not going to hack this pace that is going at Crowe Rope.

AR   No kidding. That's got to be hard. What's it look like with Thomaston?

LL   I don't know. They're hard people to deal with. That's the state for you. I had to go back for my oral review. I had passed everything else.

AR   What kind of things do they ask in the oral review?

LL   Well, if a guy sat down at the table and you asked him to remove his hat, would you insist on him removing it? Well, you've got to be careful because you could start a riot, too. So, you know, questions like that. Or someone jumped over the wall. Would you be able to shoot him?

AR   Do you think you could?

LL   I would do everything in my power to stop him before it came to that.

AR   Are they meaning, "Are you a good enough shot that you would be able to shoot him?"

LL   Oh, yes. I'm a good enough shot. . . .

AR   What would you say about the time you spent at Penobscot and what it meant to you as a job? What it meant to spend that many years working in the poultry industry in Maine?

LL   Well, it was a job. Close to home. And, of course, you made a few friends. And when it closed its doors, it meant that it not only hurt the workers there but it hurt the towns around. . . .

AR   Yeah. It's hard. There's been a lot of that through the whole country, Linda. . . . What do you think about plant closings happening like that?

LL   Well, it just shows you that times are hard. And between the union workers and OSHA, it's making it hard for the people that had a plant, about trying to keep going. And also the wages that people expected, too, it didn't help.

AR   Hmm. I've heard some cases that some plants close down not so much because they're not that profitable but often times because the company is,

Penobscot Bay, Belfast, Maine. Summer 1994.

like, doing a merger or an acquisition. Or they're selling a company and buying another because they make more money doing that. What do you think about that kind of stuff?

LL   Well, there's not much we can do about it.

AR   Yeah. What do you think businesses owe communities, if anything at all? Like Penobscot . . . , do you think they owed the town anything, or the community or people like yourself, or not?

LL   No, I don't think they owed us anything. I don't think they owed Belfast anything. It just happened to be where the business was. And the killing plant was more centrally located around the chicken farms and so forth.

AR   So your feeling is . . . if they have to close they have to close and that's just kind of the breaks for the community?

LL   Yup.

AR   Wow. Do you think it would make any difference—in your thinking any-way—if the plant wasn't really doing that badly? I mean, are there any cases in which it really would be unfair to a community for them to close down? Or do you just think they can do whatever they want to do?

LL   I think they can do more or less what they want to do. Because they're the ones that have got to pay a large sum of money on insurance. They've got to pay taxes. . . . And your wages. So, you know, if a company has got to pay out a lot and they're not making that much in return—

AR   Right. What about if they are making a profit, but they sell because they're making more money somewhere else, doing something else? How do you feel about that?

LL   [Pause] Well, that's part of life. It really is. Of course, they're thinking about money and where they can get cheaper labor and so forth. Try to keep going.

[In a later phone conversation, on April 5, 1995, when I asked Linda to clarify whom she felt was responsible in the case of U.S. industries moving abroad, she said she thought that both business and government should be trying to keep industry in this country, implying that businesses do owe something to the communities in which they operate.]

AR   Do you think Penobscot could have stayed open? Do you think the poultry industry could have survived in Maine?

LL   Hmm. Yes and no. See, what hurt us was the electricity up here for the winter, shipping the grain. But I think if we could have gone into making TV dinners and stuff—or, you know, cooking chicken that can warm up in the microwave—I think we might have been able to keep going a little bit longer. . . .

It's just the economy is real hard, and I can't see that it's any better now than it was when Penobscot closed. Sooner or later there has got to be a turnaround. There's got to be someone that's going to start thinking about getting working people—get back here in Maine and set up a business and keep people working instead of being on welfare.

AR   Whose responsibility do you think that is?

LL   For one, I think the governor has a lot to do with it.

AR   Who got in office [during the 1994 election]?

LL   King. . . . He's someone that was an independent and he happened to win. He claims he's going to help the working people. We'll see what happens. . . .

AR   Anything else you'd like to add about Penobscot or about your life now?

LL   Life is one hard struggle. But it would be wherever you are. Everything goes up but your wages. . . . I think it's about time that they stop—the State of Maine would have a lot more money if they'd stop handing out for welfare and stuff like that. I think they need to get these people off of welfare and get them into some kind of a job.

AR   What would you do if you were governor?

LL   I would do my power to try to draw industries in to the state of Maine. Try to cut down on taxes and stuff. You know, kind of give them a break if they set up a business.

AR   Yeah, I've heard actually that when a plant leaves a town that the taxes have to get absorbed by the town, and that ends up getting really costly. So that it costs both on the end of them coming in, and then if they go out all of a sudden.

LL Yeah, yeah. What do you think about right there in Belfast, last year they were crying because people weren't paying their taxes? But how can they? There's no jobs. And, of course, you've got the school that you're taxed for, and then you've got people that are on welfare that it's taxed on the working people. It just makes it hard, for the working people.

AR Yeah. . . . What kind of changes have happened for you in your life in the last six years since Penobscot closed?

LL Well, I've lost the parents, that's all. And you just struggle trying to make ends meet, pay your bills. . . .

AR Yeah. What's your community like these days? Who are you spending time with?

LL Oh, I have a few friends. You know, like the Gallaghers, Annie and Bobby Stimpson. But, you know, there's a lot of things to do around here, so I don't get out that much, unless I play [drums]. . . . And then I've got my trike [motorcycle] I ride around in the summer.

AR [Pause] Well, are you going to stay in Maine, Linda?

LL I guess so. My roots are here.

AR How much does that affect your decision to stay in Maine? Having roots?

LL Quite a lot. But if worse came to worse, I could always rent the place out and, you know, go.

AR But do you think you'd ever really do that? Would you really leave Maine?

LL If I really *had to*—to find a job—yes. Otherwise, I'm content. I'm a country girl. . . .

AR So if working for a living is just to bring the dollars in, what are the areas of your life that you do get enjoyment from and that do mean a lot to you?

LL Well, I love my animals. And I've got my trike and my motorcycle. And I like to hunt, and I like to fish, and I like to camp. I don't have much of a chance now, but I used to way back. And I just love nature.

    [We talk about Maine and about my having moved to North Carolina.]

AR Carolyn talks about how . . . people are encouraged to go get education and leave their communities. And she thinks that that ends up affecting communities not always in the best way. . . . What do you think about that?

LL Well, she's right. But also they're going where the money is. They're going out of state where they can get a better paying job and so forth.

AR Yeah. It seems like a lot of times when you talk about things, you talk about both sides of it. . . . Is that part of how you just see life?

LL Yup.

AR Kind of your own philosophy?

LL Right.

Linda with her dogs, Tippy and Bandit, in front of the home where she grew up and in which she currently lives, Brooks, Maine. Summer 1994.

AR   So are you content or not content? [laughs]

LL   Well, the only thing is, you'd like to find a good paying job, where you haven't got to struggle to make ends meet. But, of course, that's what life is all about. In a lot of ways, I'm content. I mean, I've got the place up here now. And I'm out of town. But it isn't much fun living by yourself either. But otherwise I'm getting by. That's the main thing. Been lucky. I've got a job, which a lot of people don't.

Essays

Epilogue

Faces in the Hands

CAROLYN CHUTE

THERE WAS THIS PARTY I WAS AT RECENTLY. I WAS on one end of a couch . . . a teal-colored couch, I think it was. I was picking from a platter of cheeses and pickles and olives and little cupcakes. A young man in a pastel shirt and pastel pants sat beside me, and we began to chat. After only a few moments of chatting, he let it be known that he was an engineer with a company. I let my eyes give him a little quick once-over, and it was plain he didn't mean the smiling waving train engine kind. He tells me about some people employed by his company, that they "have the gall to be asking for higher pay and some more benefits." They weren't like him, he assured me. They were machine operators. "Just a pair of hands," said he with a simper.

Hands body-less against space?

My eyes now did a little quickie once-over of my own hands, hands that had worked the factories. *Had* these hands been body-less, soulless against the background of the great American business? My right hand fetched a cute green-tinted cupcake and stuffed it into my mouth. What could I say to this professional who to the wide world glowed so pastel and perfect pink in his successfulness? I squinted at my hands again, dumbfounded.

My brother, a weightlifter, was Mr. Maine awhile ago. During that year, a new magazine for business people hit the mails. One of its first issues featured an article on what they called "the Maine work ethic." Is the Maine work ethic really dead? Experts discussed whether or not Maine people enjoyed backbreaking, boring work as much as they used to. Even with all the "experts," the general feeling of the article was puzzlement . . . though an uplifting and sunshiney resolution was tacked on in the final paragraph. The magazine's glossy cover showed my brother's arm body-less against a black background. "Gosh," I marveled, reaching for a couple of olives. Is that arm truly the way the pastel-dress jacket-necktie people see the worker who makes their business possible? Is this why it's okay for so many to pay their workers wages that won't cover a month's rent? Would they pay less if they could? If it weren't for unions and the minimum wage (obscenely small as that is), would businesses pay anything at all? Is it easier to exploit people who are faceless? "Yep," I said aloud around my mouthful of olives. The engineer glanced with a startled expression at my mouth. I reached for a pickle.

Just a pair of hands. Yep. How about just a stomach? That's what I was once . . . just a stomach, body-less against space, working on the bridge of a potato harvester . . . lurching about on a windy field, a sort of gray and stormy sea . . . my stomach body-less against space on the verge of throwing up . . . hour after hour . . . day after day. And where the harvester got stuck in the mud, the potatoes were not potatoes coming your way, but a gluey, putrid, white stench. I quit. The Maine work ethic wasn't on my mind that day. Having no mind . . . just a stomach. You know, it's like that with any pain or punishment . . . impossible to get your elevated thoughts together with such distractions.

Then it was the chicken factory. Each morning it was like a knife to my heart to leave my cooking, sewing, sweeping, wash-hanging . . . my beloved home and my little daughter. At the factory the grease of the yellowy cooked meat streaked my face and gave my hair an unnatural thickness. Sealed over with grease and the roaring thrumming heat, the meat and I were one.

And so the days passed . . . identical. As the soggy golden matter chugged by on the conveyor belt and my hands flew, I would daydream of the coming weekend, which seemed a hundred years away. Or of early mornings standing at the bathroom sink brushing my daughter Joannah's hair into two ponytails, knotting green yarn bows on them to match her green dress . . . or red to match her sailor dress . . . or blue to go with jeans. Against my fingers was *not* the chicken meat but her yellow hair, an aureate braille. Hands when they are placed on a child are not hands in space but hands connected to your past, to your future, to eternity. It's a powerful incentive to have more babies. The less rewarding your job is, the more important children become. Children are your individual creations, singular and intricate. A child is the ultimate masterpiece.

Back at the party, the engineer on the teal-colored couch beside me is telling me more about his career. He's using one hand to gesture, and I take note that the palm and five fingers are pink and silky as lips.

Meanwhile, back at the chicken factory I was pondering what I was going to do on payday. Times had changed, prices had swelled, but the paycheck stayed eensie. And there were more and more things our legislators, town hall authorities, school authorities, insurance companies, and neighbors said we had to have. It's the law that you and your kids and your yard and your vehicle LOOK nice, laws of one kind or another. Dress codes, building codes, mandatory liability insurance, mandatory this, mandatory that . . . lawmakers always being so quick to legislate you a new expense, so slow to raise the minimum wage . . . and neighbors with their eye on you . . . garage mechanic looking under your car . . . everybody pointing at you . . . rusty this and rusty that . . . two weeks pay for an exhaust system, two weeks pay for your overdue liability insurance . . . cops squinting at your car, code man squinting at your house, teachers squinting at your kids, neighbors squinting, peering, gloating, "Got a backed up septic system, huh? Better get it fixed quick!" It was hard enough being able to afford not to be an outlaw, let alone afford luxuries like house payments, health insurance, gasoline, dish detergent, propane to heat the water and cook with, doctor bills and dentist bills that insurance wouldn't cover even if you *had* insurance, lightbulbs, shoes for my girl, food, toilet paper. Maybe I could sneak a roll of toilet paper from the chicken factory ladies' room. But they got ahead of me on that. They know how to deal with outlaws and thieves. They had the tissue dispenser locked.

Now and then the bosses would stroll through the plant to check up on things. When they did this, I know they saw my face as no different from the vacant dead stare of the electrically stunned upside-down chickens with their throats cut, dangling along toward their predestined forms: chicken spread, chicken dog food, chicken hotdogs. But behind my dead eyes my brain saw the way my kitchen looked at home, yellow cat curled in the sun on a chair, and the born and unborn children of all time flashing by, the voice that is the family trait, the nose of my father's side, the smile of my mother's side, the precise and yet ethereal possible cries of "Mumma!" and "Mumma!" and "Mumma!" while on and on my hands tore the hot chicken muscle from bones and bosses passed to the next operation, satisfied.

The Maine work ethic. What the hell is that anyway, as opposed to the Rhode Island work ethic? Consider this quote from John Poor of Andover, Massachusetts, a railroad visionary: "The capacity of the human frame for labor is found to be greater in Maine than Massachusetts or any other state, south or west of it."

Having some North Carolina blood coming in on my father's side must have been why I was getting weary of the chicken factory life. I just couldn't seem to feel that great noble surge, that "Hi-ho! Hi-ho! It's off to work we go!" frame of mind as I chugged along in my outlaw car from my outlaw home, running out of gasoline along the way, scouting for unattended-looking gas stations that might not have their toilet paper dispensers locked.

What by gorry is *any* kind of work ethic? Is it work for the sake of work? In the dictionary, the word *ethic* is described as "moral duty." Duty to whom? Wasn't it Thomas Jefferson who said an industrialized nation cannot be a true democracy?

What was it like here before industrialism? Before technology-ism, computer-ism, shopping-mall-ism, business-meeting-and-banquet-at-a-nice-hotel-ism?

When we were an agricultural people, the farm, the home, the family was the product. This was your masterpiece. You watched it grow or fail. A new season might bring renewed hope if you failed last year. Life was full of surprises. Suspense. Broken tools. Broken bones. Bad weather. Insects. Work. Work. Work. Passion. Ideas. Big ideas. Good ideas. Bad ideas. Traditions. Surprises, more surprises. Pride. The whole family . . . mother and father, teens and babies, an uncle and maybe a couple of burly aunts, everybody together battling away at the godly and ungodly forces that trickled out food, water, heat. Family with one goal in common . . . the finish line, the home plate . . . the harvest, the woodpile, the *home*.

Of course, not everybody liked farming. But in those days if you got caught out behind the barn with a book, you might get the strap. Reading a book was goofing off. Funny how fashion goes, isn't it? Who is it that decides these things?

Family units. Life in common. Work in common. Misery in common.

Families are not necessary to industry. But work for the sake of work is necessary to industry.

If we, Maine, we, America, are going to have a *true* free enterprise system in the future, we're going to have to think seriously of why the work ethic is dying and if there ever was one.

And "family." Are we going to see the extinction of *that* "system"?

Will we someday be little more than individual ants with one great corporate queen-ant biz dictating from the top?

Another cupcake . . . chocolate with white nonpareils. And the voice from the other side of the couch chatting away about his latest project. But what is there for me to reply to this person who will not really ever know me, he a person who cannot understand anything but the academic A plus. My thoughts must remain my own this evening.

So whose babies *are* the mills? *Somebody* must love them. The owners, of course. The owners love their mills, dream of them all night. They feel a thrill over mills. Passion. Joy. Consternation. Challenge. Surprises. Incentive. Pride. They have a *great* sense of the work ethic. They bounce out of bed each morning to work on that baby, to make it grow and to keenly dwell on that margin of profit and to ask, "What's the matter with the workers? How come they don't work harder? And harder and harder? What's all this complaining about wanting more pay? How come they don't love my mill, my masterpiece, my baby?"

I quit that chicken-picking job, too. I do not have enough Maine work ethic. I am not a good person. I am not a good American. I went on welfare, which is even worse. Welfare people are lazy nocounts living off the dole, they say.

Years later, on the teal-colored couch, checking out more pickles, sweet and dill, one of each, I am wondering, what about businesses that quit the people? Especially the ones that move somewhere else to find cheaper and cheaper, more desperate help. Leaving the state. Leaving the country. Where's *their* moral duty? *Their* patriotism?

And what about these big businesses that get the dole?

Why does the obligation, the duty, always wind up in the lap of the individual, the worker, and never, NEVER the big guys? And how come comfy Joe and Jane America, the ones who are themselves workers but somewhat better paid workers, are always so quick to blame higher prices, higher taxes, job shortages, and what-all on the lower paid worker or the out-of-work worker and sometimes the better paid union worker . . . but never do they blame the boss, the owner, Mr. Biz?

"Joe and Jane are worried," I mutter around a dill pickle. "Yep, that's it. They are worried sick by the terrible power of the great punishing Dad . . . Dad who is America, God, and Wealth . . . especially Wealth, for if you don't pray to it enough and honor and obey it, it won't trickle down. If you question its holiness, things might get seriously worse for you."

"Excuse me?" wonders the man in pastel on the couch beside me, looking with narrowed, bewildered eyes at my mouth. Was I thinking aloud again? I reach for a little embossed napkin and wipe the pickle juice from my fingers.

Our neighbor Glen stops by for tea sometimes. Stepping out of his truck, he always has that same embarrassed look most Mainers have these days having to drive around with VACATIONLAND and red lobsters on both front and back bumpers. Glen is a carpenter and does some work in the woods, logs and pulp, firewood. He is building his own house, a farm, he tells us . . . the slow old-fashioned few-boards-at-a-time way, the no-bank-loan way, the you-don't-get-it-all-at-once way. He is independent, thoughtful. With a tea mug in one hand, he gives his mustache a few deep-thought pulls with the other. He says he's been thinking about why workers in some places, like those plants in the Midwest that make cars, are never happy with their paychecks and benefits, even when they have pretty good paychecks, at least by the standards we Maine workers know. He says he thinks the reason is because no matter how much they make, they have this unexpressed knowing that they are possessed, owned. Body and soul. They know what they'll be doing tomorrow. They know what they'll be doing next week. Next year. They can see their lives stretching out before them unvaried, flat, and uniform. They have already lived their future. They are the living dead. Carcasses, if not slaves. What price would you put on your life? The price is never good enough.

And yet what does the business owner vow to you? That plant can shut you out tomorrow, leave you fifty-five years old and jobless.

Something moves. Gives me a start. It's the young engineer on the couch beside me, reaching for a pink cupcake. He turns it in his long fingers and asks, "What do *you* do?"

"Blipe," I say around a big bite of very sunshiney yellow cupcake. And another olive. I chew thoughtfully, nodding, smiling, stalling. I'm wondering if the engineer has children. But of course. It's his privilege. It's the low-pay people who aren't supposed to have kids. You hear it time and time again: "And there they were in that dumpy place with all those kids. Argh!" or "After a person *that* poor has more kids than she can afford, you start taking the kids away."

How come nobody threatens to take away the kids of the employer who pays his people too little? Why don't *those* types stop having kids? Look what their kind has made this world into? Look at their high-pay, high-profit waste. They are smashing the world.

I am remembering Reuben. Am I enraged by his death? Or content? I want to tell you about Reuben, but first I have to tell you about his people, my people.

One of the things I admire most about my husband, Michael, is his hands. I remember when I met him in a darkish lakeside barroom, even while falling in love with his voice and eyes, his beard, his lanky, sinewy height, my eyes scrutinized those hands. I remember thinking, yes, those are the hands, the hands of my people.

My people. Memories filled with hands. My grandfather died when I was eighteen. I was terrified of the "viewing room," where you stand around the open casket. I stayed out in the anteroom with my cousin Jane. Jane's father was my grandfather's brother, Jim. Jim had died young. Jim dug bait worms for a living in Belfast. When we went to Belfast to visit, I remember my aunt's hands breaking open clams in the slate sink. Jim took us kids to the shed. I'll never forget him unbolting the shed door and there, living in wet hay, was the prize, the longest stinging bait worm he'd ever dug. It looked like a red snake with legs. I was impressed.

Jim was dying even then. Later he spent most of his time in a chair in the kitchen. His black, black hair was long because he was too sick to have it cut, our aunt told us apologetically on one of our last visits before he died. But I thought that hair was the most beautiful thing, back in those days when you never saw anybody's true hair, back in those days of buzzers and crewcuts. I remember holding my eyes on him, dazzled. He was part Indian, death in his eyes, his hands in his lap.

After my grandfather's funeral, on the ride home, my mother said, "You were right, Carolyn, not to want to see him. It didn't look like him at all." She sighed. "Except his hands . . . his beautiful hands." I could see clearly the short fingers, one with a "claw," and his wedding ring . . . how he always bragged he had never taken that ring off since it was put there. Not ever. By the time he died, the ring was as thin as a yellow hair.

My husband, Michael, wears green workshirts and green workpants. His eyes are brown, hair black, a little long. My mother says he looks like our uncle Jim. Michael is respectful of and dazzled by all life. He has magic in his hands. I've seen him carry a spider to safety. Another time a mouse. I have a photograph of Michael with a butterfly calmly settled on one of his thumbs. He has a volunteer job these days. He takes meals around to old folks. Some days he goes back and spends afternoons with them. He feeds their pets for them. The old guys and Michael shoot the breeze. They cover woods, weather, guns, and other country stuff. Michael can only write his first and last name, not his middle name. He can't read my name at all. His pay job these days is mowing graves. Makes $1,000 a year thereabouts.

Back in school Michael was called dumb by a lot of his teachers. Some called him a troublemaker. One of them put him out in the hall every day in third grade. Later he went to a fate worse than the hallway. SPECIAL ED, OR "RETARD ED," as some of the kids called it. Just because of dyslexia, because words scrambled on the page before his eyes, he was scolded, jeered, punished, stigmatized.

Back then, even then, Michael loved old people, had a way with them . . . aunt, uncle, grandmother, gramp were what life was about to Michael. But public school doesn't give you a grade in OLD PEOPLE. That's not ACADEMIC enough. It's not a thing you can do at your desk. And now in adulthood, Michael finds his greatest gift is still not valued. Helping old people is not a product. It's not a thing rich people can buy shares in. So his talents will never earn him a paycheck. In the eyes of America, Michael is still a failure.

We had mixed feelings back when we discovered I was pregnant with Reuben. The world was not exactly waiting for Reuben with open arms. But I studied the prenatal pamphlets showing fetuses at all stages of growth, trying to imagine Reuben's face, cell by cell, our masterpiece.

If I slammed the door of our old truck or dropped a kettle lid, Reuben would startle inside me, jerking back his hands and feet. Other times he would yearn up toward his father's spread hand.

It was in the days when President Ronald Reagan was riding his horse and talking softly into the microphone and many people were mesmerized. "He will cut those lazy types off without a dime!" good-pay Americans cheered. "And then those lazy bums will have to get themselves REAL jobs."

I overheard a neighbor snorting, "The president will clean up the garbage" and rolled his eyes toward my pregnant belly.

People who heard I was on welfare, people who had good-pay jobs, said, "Why doesn't Mike get a better job? Why doesn't he get two jobs? Three jobs? When I was young, I worked twelve hours a day, six days a week for fifteen dollars a week, and *I* didn't complain, *I* didn't ask for welfare." Sometimes they said, "Why doesn't Mike get his high school diploma? You can't amount to anything without that."

Once, when someone said this, Michael's hands tightened in rage. He went to the bureau drawer, found his high school diploma, gave it a toss into the woodstove, and said gravely, "I've wanted to do that for a long time."

The unborn baby grew big. On both sides of the family, nice big babies were the usual.

Meanwhile, Michael was at the dairy farm or the orchard, pruning apple trees, harvesting potatoes, or splitting other people's firewood . . . moving from job to job . . . salvage yard, gardening, cold storage work, jobs that didn't require him to read and write . . . jobs that didn't depend on self-esteem. Jobs that paid minimum wage or less.

Meanwhile, President Reagan was riding his horse and tipping his hat, and the good-pay Americans were cheering as he cut money to the states and as the state of Maine took away my medical card, which was giving me and my baby medical care that Michael's check wouldn't cover.

Meanwhile, industries were leaving Maine, the great conveyor belts silenced, the truck bays and loading docks empty . . . chicken . . . shoes . . . textiles. Gone. Everybody scrambling to grab up what was left of the jobs.

The governor said not to worry. New jobs were on the way. Tourism was coming. You'll have lots of jobs soon. We tried to grin and bear the VACATIONLAND red lobster license plates. Some tried to grin and bear the new tourist-related jobs that were always part-time jobs and that offered low pay and no benefits. People even grinned through seeing the tourists who decided to STAY and live in Maine where *life is as it ought to be* . . . tourists whose willingness to pay *any* price skyrocketed the price of a home . . . a price low-pay working people could not afford and better-pay working people *thought* they *could* afford, going into debt neck-deep.

Everybody was grinning.

They told Michael, "Go get a job at McDonalds."

"Raise your aspirations," said others. Educators especially. They love that word. ASPIRATIONS. All over the state you can hear that long word rolling off their tongues. It's something the low-income people don't have enough of, they say.

Aspirations???

Where are the little farms? A person with learning disabilities who wasn't born to be a pastel-shirt person could get by with his own little farm . . . could be *interde-pendent* . . . could practice Yankee ingenuity and good Yankee sense. The farm . . . the farm . . . just a fading whisper . . . gone.

And now the mills. Going.

The governor says what we need is more tourist-related jobs. We should bring in more tourists. But then sometimes the governor says tourist-related jobs are bad. What's the matter with you people? Can't you raise your aspirations? The governor tells the schools to give the kids more homework and longer school days to help them raise their aspirations and get them out of those dead-end tourist jobs.

Somebody tells Michael, "Raise your aspirations! Computers are the thing!"

Everything's getting fast, faster. Keep up or keep out. "That's life," the politicians say. "If you can't keep up, you fall by the wayside. Fact of life."

Meanwhile, with no welfare medical card, I lost my private doctor. The prenatal clinic I went to was crammed with those fallen by the wayside of the president's and the governor's cuts. The hospital was crammed . . . so crammed that I was in labor with a breech birth baby for two weeks and a temperature of 104 degrees before the hospital would let me in.

His name was Reuben. Thick auburn hair. Narrow-shouldered. Dehydrated. Starved. He is buried here in these hills among his ancestors going back 150 years, the farmers of small farms and their great independence and pride. When I visit his grave, I am content. I tell him I'm glad he's dead. Safe. Spared. I say, "Dear, dear Reuben . . . dear gentle person. What if you were born?"

Well, there he goes again. The governor is on the radio talking higher aspirations for us all . . . more homework, more school hours, more, more, more! That'll cure the problem, he assures us. Doesn't he realize that the higher the white-shirt pastel-people raise their aspirations for us who are already failing *their* idea of success, the more we lose sight of our own true aspirations and the deeper into complete failure they leave us?

Reuben, dear gentle person, maybe you inherited the learning disabilities of your father and me. Maybe your talents would have been unmarketable. Maybe you would have had to take time and care with everything you would do. Schools and jobs have no patience. Maybe by the time you were a man, you couldn't feel like a man. You'd break one of their laws. And soon there are going to be A LOT MORE LAWS . . . school classrooms packed like cattle pens, prisons full of people standing shoulder-to-shoulder, more capital punishment, capital punishment for lesser crimes to make room, more drugs, lots more drugs, more disease, less help from doctors, people getting mad, people in mobs . . . everybody falling by the wayside . . . no place for the gentle, old-fashioned people . . . room only for the high-aspirations people. "Better people." Better, smarter, cleaner, spotless, odorless, hair that doesn't seem like hair, skin that doesn't smell like skin, hands and fingernails that are silky as lips, humanity with no trace of mammalhood but uniformly glib with accent-free voices. Such creatures! Polymerized, preserved, freed of flaw, soaring up, up, up, and away . . . the ultimate win.

Something shifts on the couch beside me. I see the pastel-shirt pastel-pants fellow is still admiring his pink cupcake, but he doesn't eat it. He is telling me about something "incredible" he has just read in the *New York Times* this week.

Meanwhile, at the Blaine House (fancy mansion the governor lives in), the governor is probably helping himself to a snack before the maids bring supper. With his right hand he reaches for a cracker, applies soft cheese with a knife, leans back into his chair, and nibbles. His hands brush crumbs from his pastel dress pants. Governors everywhere reaching. And the president. Not the one on the horse; now it's the one with the big gas-guzzling boat. He is perhaps in his office this evening, leaning back in his big groaning chair with wheels, reaching, munching. President munching. Governors munching. Hands brushing crumbs to the rug.

You hear it these days . . . a lot of talk about choices . . . good choices, bad choices. You are shepherds of your own destiny, they say. There are how-to books on making the right choices. There are high-price counselors you can go sit with to help you pick the right life.

Doesn't luck play into this game somewhere? Like having the great big good luck of having what you are naturally good at be marketable, highly paid, highly respected.

But the idea of luck might take away the moral aspect of things, the idea that good people make the right choices, bad people make bad choices, and people get what they deserve.

Work hard, you win. Goof off, you lose. This is the belief.

The words of yesteryear's Maine were WORKING TOGETHER. The word today is COMPETITION. Like sports. Like school spirit. Whose baby is reading first? Whose school has the better team of better babies? Whose SAT tests are higher? Whose school puts out more professional types, fewer flunk-outs? Whose country does? Are we beating the Russians with more smart, more knowledgeable, more high-drive graduates? Beating the Japanese? Whose country has, if not more work ethic, bigger tanks, bombs, rockets, nuke subs, cruise missiles, and various other winged monstrosities . . . in case the smarter, better, faster babies of other countries get too smart or just too big and pushy, too crowded, too used up in resources, or too greedy, too "crazy"?

Our leaders and experts are always saying about the low-pay people, "They've got to break the cycle." As if the low-pay people are the ones totally in control of the situation here. What about the leaders' and experts' cycles of greed and waste? And ignorance? Especially ignorance. Gosh, how *little* they know!

"Low-income people have got to escape," they say. Escape what? Do they mean *leave home*? Leave town? Like they did? Do they mean escape that life we have here in Maine with our family ties and hometown ties and go to . . . to . . . to Harvard or Yale, like they did? Live in a faraway city? Be a yuppie? Is that the only acceptable choice? Why was it so easy for *them* to leave *their* homes, these leaders, these experts, these professionals? Were their homes dysfunctional in a way social workers aren't trained to recognize?

And besides, I thought Maine was *where life is as it should be*.

Maybe by "escape" they mean something along the lines of . . . get out of the way. Like a long time ago when they gave the Maine natives reservations to live on. What do they have in mind for us this time? Cement block public housing?

Back then, were they telling the Maine folks (the Passamaquoddies and Penobscots), "You have choices. You are the shepherds of your own destinies. The reservation or Harvard—take your pick."

Down at the pub for pizzas, Michael and I see some of the box shop guys who have been laid off . . . some woolen mill folks . . . and those who work in the woods . . . talking weather, sports, war, and the god-awful price of a can of Spam. The light from the table lamps on these men's hands is yellow and fuzzy and forgiving. Their hands, like their faces, are expressing glee or rage. One of them has a short finger. One of them has a couple of short fingers and a fingernail like a claw. I look across the table at my husband's hands and at his dark green workshirt buttoned in a formal way at his throat. His hands on the table are empty. But to me and to many, he is the axis of the earth.

Meanwhile, the governors unfold their cloth napkins and pick up pretty forks. The open newspaper tells of some of the doings of the low-pay people OUT THERE . . . the trials and tribulations they cause, their peculiarities, their discontent . . . distant . . . distant beings . . . as distant as if on a small blue planet in the black firmament. "What the hell is going on with these low-income types?" the president wonders. "What are we going to do about the mess they cause?" And the governors scratch their heads. In their respective mansions, they reach for the crusty bread.

I turn. The engineer is waiting for me to say something. Here's my chance. Should I explain, "Dear young fellow, in the hands of the working people, I've seen life, death, patience, enduring patience, surrender, miracles, and mistakes. Working people are as human as you are. They need to eat and sleep and stay warm and have a doctor when they need one, just like you do." Or should I say, "If the queen bee were alone, she'd die. All of us humans working together are a perfect thing, a human network of needs and gifts. Boss and worker, each is a gift to the other."

No, the truth is that there are too many people today . . . indeed . . . too many. In each other's way. Grabbing. Clawing. Overlapping. War and disease are ready to do nature's task . . . to cut us down. And as in employment, so in war and disease, the working people and out-of-work people, not the A plus people, will bear most of the blows. Survival of the fittest is still the great law of the land. *The Capitalist creed.*

The truth is, I'm not looking at the young engineer's face. "You seen one yuppie, you seen 'em all," some say. I want to close my eyes to the fear and hate that rises in me. There is nothing he and I have to say to each other. Diplomatic talks only take place between two powers. Not one power and one powerless. And maybe he's not all that powerful anyway, just one small-time yuppie . . . just a guy trying to get through another party, another day.

I narrow my eyes on his right hand. It's not the future I see in this man's hands. It's just a pink cupcake.

The Closing of Penobscot Poultry

ALICIA J. ROUVEROL

> CC   *Have those people talked to you about how they feel*
> *about the plant closing?*
>
> LL   *We all felt bad. I mean, after a while I guess it was*
> *just like home, right?*

THIS BOOK IS NOT ONLY LINDA LORD'S STORY. IT is also a story about the closing of Penobscot Poultry, as told by Linda. What she says about the plant closing, about her job search, about job retraining, reflect not only her own experiences on the heels of a shutdown but that of many others affected by this nationwide trend toward deindustrialization.

Defined as a systematic decline in manufacturing jobs, deindustrialization is occurring not only in the Frost Belt, from New England to the industrial Midwest, but also in the Sun Belt, across the South, and throughout the southwestern United States.[1] In the 1950s, 33 percent of American workers were employed in manufacturing. By the 1980s, that figure had dropped to 20 percent. By the early 1990s, manufacturing employed only 17 percent, with the percentage continuing to slip.[2] "Downsizing in America," a 1996 series of articles in the *New York Times*, makes plain that corporate, white-collar jobs have also been impacted.[3] Clearly, declining traditional industries and the flight of industry abroad affect us all.

Linda's mixed response to the plant's closing offers us important insights into the effects of industrial decline. At one moment, Penobscot's demise spelled disaster; at the next, relief. The townspeople of Belfast were likewise torn over the closing. Some residents, primarily newcomers, were pleased to see the departure of an unsightly and dirty industry; others, mostly longtime residents, were alarmed by its demise. As journalist and Belfast resident Jay Davis commented, "When Penobscot closed, I think a lot of us thought the sky was going to fall. Which it didn't, thankfully."[4] The plant's closing significantly affected many lives, though, and marked a shift for the region. Linda's particular experience reveals not only the impact on one community member but also the unique challenges women face in industrial decline. Such close-grained studies are critical, for it is on the local level that deindustrialization is perhaps least studied and best understood.[5]

When Penobscot Poultry closed its doors in 1988, Linda Lord and over 400 employees lost their jobs, as did 300–400 workers who were employed in related industries in the surrounding area.[6] Yet declining industries were nothing new for Waldo

Poultry barn near Brooks, Maine. February 1988.

County. A brief look at the history of the county and the poultry industry's development will tell us much about the context in which Penobscot Poultry flourished and then fell. Might Penobscot Poultry—or the industry as a whole—have survived? If the plant's demise could have been avoided, what does this tell us about a business's responsibility to the community in which it operates—especially in today's global market? Ultimately, we might ask: how do we balance the needs of business (for maximum profits) with the needs of community (for sustainable economies)? How do we resolve our contradictory or paradoxical goals? Or can we?

Poultry as a home-based operation has deep roots in Waldo County. But as an industry, broiler processing in the county grew and declined in less than fifty years. It was, moreover, only one in a series of agricultural-based industries that disappeared over the course of a single generation.

Situated in Maine's midcoast region, today Waldo County stretches 724 square miles to the west in a roughly hewn quadrangle, across hills and ridges, fields, woods, and lowlands. Water is abundant in the county; large lakes, small ponds, and streams abound. Penobscot Bay and the island of Islesboro mark the county's eastern boundary, a sweeping coastline that boasts some of the bay's best natural harbors and draws tens of thousands of tourists and "summer people" every year. Some thirty thousand inhabitants live clustered in the county's twenty-five small towns, in the city of Belfast, and along the edges of the back roads that run like ribbons over the landscape. Interstate 95 looms to the north and west, but Route 1 on the coast is the main traffic artery. Tourist and service-oriented roadside attractions dot the coastline. Inland, small, family-owned farms predominate, with fields of corn, hay, and alfalfa, pastures and woodlands butting up against the country stores replete with gas pumps and video rentals. Until recently, most of these farms specialized in poultry and dairy production.[7] While dairy farming continues, the poultry barns, hatcheries, and grain mills— former suppliers to the broiler-processing industry—now stand empty, a reminder of an industry that once thrived in the county.

In 1730, Brigadier General Samuel Waldo first secured the "Muscongus Grant" (later called the "Waldo Patent"), but settlement in the county did not begin until 1759.[8] Waldo recruited immigrants from Scotland, Ireland, Germany, and New England, who worked primarily in lumbering and fishing.[9] By 1770, Belfast was growing as a shipping center for the young lumber industry.[10] From the 1820s to the 1860s, the county experienced a remarkable boom. Lumbering flourished and peaked; canneries and clothing manufacturing developed. Maine led the way in shipbuilding, producing over a third of the nation's tonnage in 1855.[11] Agriculture flourished.[12] With an influx of new settlers, the county's population peaked in 1850 at 47,000 and has never been equaled.[13]

From the 1860s to the early 1900s, the economy of Waldo County gradually declined, as the county's virgin forests were timbered out and the shipping industry waned, and as settlers left for more fertile soil in the Midwest. Fishing and farming remained the chief occupations. Lime and granite quarries opened, tanneries and shoe factories started up, and clothing manufacturing continued. An exclusive summer colony developed on the island of Islesboro, drawing wealthy residents of Boston, New York, and Philadelphia. And finally, cheese factories developed and egg production grew, laying the groundwork for the poultry industry to expand.[14]

A number of factors influenced the development of Maine's poultry industry, including the availability of small dairy farms (with barns that could easily be converted into poultry housing) and the state's proximity to larger population centers.[15] Maine's cool climate was considered favorable, as was the state's leadership in poultry research.[16] In fact, the relative success of the industry depended in part on Maine's aggressive disease control program. But low land prices and the availability of people willing to work in poultry also supported the industry's rise.[17]

In 1860, the "chicken business" in Maine focused almost exclusively on egg production. By the 1920s, chickens were either sold locally or hauled directly to city markets by truck.[18] And by the 1930s, farmers with 2,000 to 3,000 birds could make a good living selling their live birds to out-of-state poultry buyers.[19] Virtually all processing at this time was "New York dressed": the birds were slaughtered and defeathered, but the head, feet, and innards remained. During this time, many of the poultry buyers, families such as the Lipmans, the Mendelsons, and the Savitzes, opened processing plants in Maine.[20] These poultry entrepreneurs arrived in Waldo County at a critical time, just as state and federal regulations on slaughtering and milk storage were forcing many local farmers out of business; the development of the industry saved many a family farm.[21] The poultry businessmen contracted with the farmers to raise the chickens, provided them with chicks and feed, and then took the birds back for processing.[22] The fledging industry developed both during and after World War II, fed by technological developments and heightened market demand. The federal government encouraged poultry production, purchasing large quantities of poultry to sat-isfy military needs. As a result, poultry processors gained solid profits. By 1954, poul-try was Maine's largest and most important agricultural crop.[23]

After World War II, market demand for eviscerated poultry contributed to the decline of New York dressed birds. The ultimate effect was a boom-and-bust cycle that led to a highly concentrated industry.[24] In the 1940s, there were twenty-five proces-sors in the state. But the costs of automation and conversion drove smaller firms out of business, and by 1957 only five processors remained.[25] With two of these located in Belfast—Penobscot and Maplewood Poultry Co.—Waldo County was the center of the state's industry.

Although Maine never led the nation in poultry production, poultry was none-theless central to the state's economy, and Belfast had long been the state's "broiler capital."[26] Since the late 1940s, Belfast had been the site of one of the nation's earliest large-scale, promotional chicken barbecues in Belfast, eventually billed as the "World's Largest Outdoor Barbecue." By 1973, Belfast's annual Broiler Festival drew over ten thousand people.[27] Clearly the community saw itself as a poultry-processing center, and for Belfast, chicken was indeed big business.[28] By the early 1970s, when the industry peaked, Maplewood and Penobscot together employed some 2,500 people.[29]

Such was the environment in which Penobscot Poultry got its start in Belfast in 1949, when Al Savitz began producing New York dressed poultry. Savitz later sold out, then bought the business back with financing from the Lewis family. When Savitz died soon afterward, George and Bernard Lewis took over Penobscot. George Lewis had had a successful career in fish and meat processing and cold storage, as well as in real estate.[30] But as his son, Bernard, commented, the Lewises' involvement in poultry processing represented an entirely new business arena: "I want to tell you, the learning process was intense and rapid and ultimately led to where we are today."[31]

It was in 1971 that serious problems arose in Maine's broiler processor industry. That year, both Penobscot and Maplewood were charged with violating the Refuse Act of 1899 by dumping pollutants into Penobscot Bay. Maplewood, which had been in violation of the Act for years, was fined $10,500, and Penobscot was charged $2,500.[32] Again in 1971, the U.S. Department of Agriculture filed a civil suit against Maple-wood—this time for unfair and deceptive practices toward growers.[33] In 1972, the USDA discovered high levels of PCBs (polychlorinated biphenyls) in chickens from the Maplewood, Fort Halifax, and Penobscot Poultry plants.[34] Within three weeks, by order of the USDA, poultrymen destroyed 1.25 million birds.[35] The contamina-tion was eventually traced to a single batch of feed mix at a Ralston Purina mill in Thorndike, Maine.[36] In the meantime, losses to farmers and processors totaled $3 million; because of the subsequent negative publicity, sales plummeted and Maine lost important markets in neighboring states.[37]

But these were not the only economic liabilities facing the poultry industry. In 1971, the profit margin was slim and competition was fierce. Because there were too many birds on the market, prices began to fall. With high costs for grain and fuel, the mar-gins grew closer still. In 1979, Maplewood filed for bankruptcy, and by 1981, three other poultry processors in Maine had announced plans for cutbacks and eventual closings. Between 1979 and 1984, broiler production declined by 83 percent.[38] In 1987, George

Lewis died and Bernard succeeded him. In 1988, Bernard closed down Penobscot Poultry. The company had ostensibly lost $5.5 million, and Bernard's family had pressured him to sell or liquidate the company.[39]

The reasons most often cited for poultry's demise in Maine, however, include high fuel costs, the expense of shipping grain, and especially competition with southern markets, which offered cheaper labor.[40] Other factors included vertical integration, mismanagement, problematic governmental policies, and unsustainable loans. Some critics claimed that the industry did not fail but in fact fled the state.[41] Others faulted the poultry companies for not adequately reinvesting in the industry, since increasing productivity of labor and capital requires increasing levels of investment.[42] Studies of deindustrialization reveal that plants are often closed down not just because they are no longer profitable but because they are not profitable *enough*.[43] Penobscot Poultry—and Maine's broiler industry as a whole—may well fit these patterns of industrial decline.

Vertical integration—in which the processing firms controlled all aspects of the business, from hatching the chicks to delivering the dressed poultry to market—was standard practice in the industry. Many in the poultry business have argued that vertical integration was efficient and that it essentially built the industry.[44] Critics, on the other hand, suggest that integration placed a $90 million industry in the hands of only five companies and ultimately may have contributed to poultry's demise.[45]

Some criticize the poultry firms for not diversifying. Maine's broiler industry could have moved into the prepackaged convenience foods market and parts packaging and could have developed high name recognition.[46] During the 1970s, firms like Holly Farms and Tyson Foods began to upgrade their product lines, emphasizing further processing products such as deboned poultry meat, chicken franks, and precooked chicken products. Further processing brought greater profit margins and enabled firms to ride out short-term price cycles. But Maine's broiler firms continued to produce fresh whole birds and were slow or unsuccessful in developing prepackaged products to meet this rising consumer demand.[47] As a result, the state's industry missed a large share of the market: by 1972, restaurants, drive-ins, and fast food stores already accounted for 24 percent of the broiler industry.[48] In 1971—the same year that marked a downturn for Penobscot—one of the company's chief southern competitors, Perdue, also began to implement a sophisticated marketing program that made it a household name. Maine's former agriculture commissioner, Stewart Smith, recommended in 1980 that "we should take a leaf out of Frank Perdue's book."[49] Many of the nation's poultry leaders said that Perdue's campaign was the single most effective promotion in the history of the broiler industry.[50] But Maine's poultry producers either failed to recognize the significance of these shifts in the national market or were reluctant to make the investments necessary to compete in that market.[51]

Internal mismanagement also played a role in the industry's demise. A study by David Shaw Associates of Portland, for example, noted that feed costs often varied considerably between plants within close geographical proximity, pointing to the importance of management performance in maintaining a competitive edge.[52] One report on Maplewood stated that "feed ingredients were purchased by a Boston broker on a very loose, unscientific, uncontrolled, and unmonitored basis." Evidently, Maplewood did not even have a purchasing department.[53] Linda Lord also hinted that management at Penobscot had problems: "Well, there was certain people in the office who were supposed to make out a report and let him [the owner] know what's going on—which they were making it look good on paper, but it actually wasn't happening there in the plant." David Shaw Associates concluded that despite high fuel costs, high labor costs, and the costs of shipping grain, Maine's industry could have been viable; but modern aggressive management, among other factors, would be critical to reviving the industry.[54]

In addition, Maine's poultry leaders never adequately addressed the industry's chief ill, the high cost of importing grain. In 1971, Maine firms paid $4.15 more per ton for importing corn and grain than their southern competitors.[55] According to a Water Transport Association (WTA) study, a modernized system combining ship and rail transport would have reduced the costs of feed grains from 34 to 65 percent, putting Maine broiler processors back into competition with the southern markets.[56] By 1980, the problem was still not solved and Maine's broiler processors were in trouble. "The poultry industry is in bad shape because of the built-in disadvantages we've never faced, but which we could overcome," said Stewart Smith. He also warned that expenses would only increase because of rail deregulation and rising energy costs.[57] David Shaw Associates noted that "the single most important geographical cost problem to be addressed is the development of lower freight rates for feed ingredients. It is unlikely that a broiler industry of substantial size will be reestablished or continue to exist without positive progress in this area."[58] But clearly the public and private sectors never successfully solved this critical weak link in the industry.

Other problematic governmental policies took the form of "bad" loans to the industry, loans that could not be maintained. The *Maine Times* quoted Seth Bradstreet, former director of the Maine Farmers Home Administration (FmHA), as saying that his agency was often pressured by the congressional delegation to approve loans even if the situation did not merit it. By 1979, the FmHA had indirectly subsidized the Maine poultry industry for twenty-five years through low-interest loans to poultry farmers. At that time, the FmHA was financing 60 percent of the broiler housing space in Maine, while nationwide the FmHA financed only 3–10 percent. But it was not only the government which had a policy of making questionable loans to the industry. In 1978, Maplewood successfully negotiated a $1 million loan from Merrill Trust Company of Bangor and three other banks to capitalize on a supposed upturn in the market the subsequent year and to take advantage of tax laws that favored expansion. The predicted boom never took place, and by fall of 1979, Maplewood filed for bankruptcy.[59]

The final reason for poultry's demise in Maine was overproduction, which had plagued the industry for years. New vaccines may have helped to accelerate production and expand the market, since the industry was able to grow birds more quickly.[60] But overproduction can also be linked, in part, to the FmHA loan policies, which fueled the industry's expansion through the building of poultry housing. The industry overexpanded, flooding the market and driving down prices.[61]

The failure of Maine's poultry industry could not have happened at a worse time for Waldo County. By the late 1980s, the shoe industry had also collapsed, which meant that the county's two primary sources of employment had evaporated. But even before the demise of these industries, Waldo County had seen severe poverty and high unemployment. By 1980, 20 percent of its residents were living below the poverty line. From 1978 to 1985, Waldo County lost 43 percent of its manufacturing jobs. In 1985, per capita income in Waldo County was $7,021, while the state level was $9,042. By

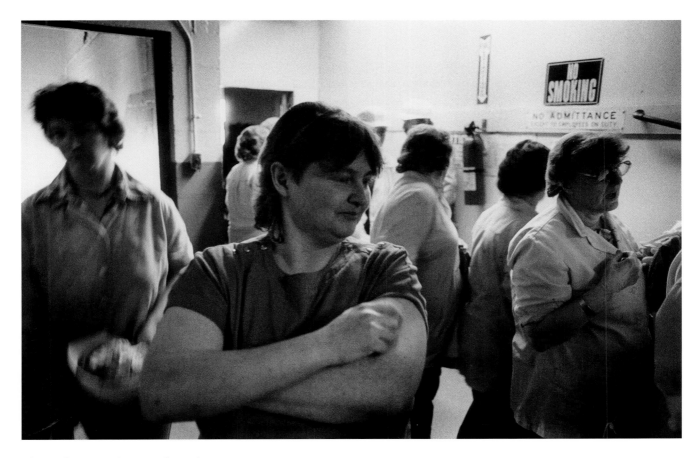

Closing day at Penobscot Poultry. February 24, 1988.

1987, Waldo County was the third poorest county in the state of Maine with a per capita income of $11,645, three-quarters of the state's average.[62] In recent years, Waldo County and the state as a whole have experienced an upturn in the economy, but most of that growth has been in the service sector, while manufacturing has declined.[63]

What does all of this mean for Waldo County? When the poultry industry failed in Maine, it followed in the wake of a host of other industries. In Waldo County, po- tato farming had peaked in the 1940s, commercial fishing in the 1950s, leather in the 1960s, and finally poultry in the 1970s. All these industries waned thereafter. Today, forest products rank number one and tourism number two in Maine's economy. Yet it is clear that Maine's economy is, and always has been, based primarily on natural resources and manufacturing—regardless of the growth of service industries. Econo- mist Richard Barringer suggests that out-of-state capital has generally fueled the state's development, that Maine has never supported its own growth, and that in fact the state banking laws do not encourage such self-support. He also notes that in about 1982— after the 1974 OPEC oil price increases—Maine, and certainly Waldo County, entered a new era. "It's not by accident that those four traditional industries have in fact met their demise in this county, some of them in the state as a whole. We're now in a new era of international competition in which this state . . . will [not] be able to compete successfully in the production of a commodity good based upon a low-wage labor. Poultry was one such commodity."[64]

Barringer's statement raises a key question: How does Penobscot's closing fit into the national and international picture? In her testimony, Linda Lord aptly describes the effects of international markets on local industries when she points out that U.S. businesses themselves—by setting up shop abroad—helped to create the international competition that led to their own demise. This may be true for shoe and car production, as she suggests, but what of poultry processing? Although Maine's poultry firms faced southern (not international) competition, I would argue that the "failure" of the Maine poultry industry may have been caused in part by capital flight *of a different kind.* And it is here that we come to see the decline of the shoe and poultry industries as microcosms of a larger trend of industrial decline, both regional and national.

Between 1967 and 1976, New England saw a 14 percent drop in manufacturing jobs.[65] In Maine, 107 plants closed between 1971 and 1981, resulting in the direct loss of 21,215 jobs. Virtually all of these were manufacturing positions.[66] Figuring both indirect and direct job loss, the total jobs lost due to these Maine plant closings totaled 49,219 for the ten-year period. As it turns out, *bankruptcy caused only 13 percent of these shutdowns.*[67] Moreover, according to a 1987 General Accounting Office report, not all bankruptcies result from failed businesses. In fact, 92 percent result from disinvestment, restructurings, "runaway plants," and the like.[68]

While political economist Barry Bluestone has defined deindustrialization as a "systematic decline in the industrial base," economists increasingly understand the phenomenon to encompass far more than the loss of our nation's manufacturing base.[69] Jobs *are* being created. The issue is the *type* of jobs created and their geographical locale. Job growth in the 1980s and early to mid-1990s was predominantly in the retail and service sectors, generally offering low pay with few benefits.[70] Statistics also show that while the share of manufactured exports produced in the United States slipped between 1955 and 1985, the percent of global production held by U.S.–owned corporations has actually increased.[71] Mexico alone has seen a dramatic rise in U.S.–owned export-oriented assembly plants (called *maquiladoras*). In 1968, there were 112 maquiladoras; by 1992, there were over 2,000.[72] U.S. corporate managers are still investing, but they are not investing in this country's basic industries.

"Runaway shops," the relocation of plants from one region to another, are not a recent phenomena, of course. As far back as the 1920s, and again in the 1950s, the shoe, textile, and apparel industries left New England for the nonunionized, lower-wage South.[73] But Barry Bluestone argues that industrial decline took on a new shape after World War II. In the affluent 1950s and 1960s, he suggests, corporations were able to maintain high profits *and* support the gains made by organized labor; they could also afford to pay for a larger share of the social safety net. But by the 1970s, corporations could no longer maintain the profits of the boom years and also maintain the social contract. Capital mobility became a key strategy for lowering costs, and redirection of investment from basic manufacturing became fundamental to increased profits.[74]

Capital mobility also takes the form of mergers, acquisitions, and foreign investment. In some cases, profits from one plant's operations are reallocated to new facilities. In other instances, plants are not necessarily closed but rather are allowed to run down; eventually a plant with outmoded equipment will no longer be sufficiently productive. Management, then, uses not only the profits from the existing operation but also its depreciation reserves to invest elsewhere. The existing plant—once it is no longer sufficiently productive or no longer meets profit targets—is bound to close.[75]

Rather than upgrading or modernizing plants, U.S. corporations have opted to maximize profits through acquisitions and speculative investments.[76] In the 1980s, the number of acquisitions and mergers reached record levels and exceeded the amount invested in new U.S. facilities and equipment. While these transactions can reap large profits for investors and create enormous commissions for those directly involved, they often encourage little or no real economic growth.[77]

The fate of Penobscot Poultry, in some ways at least, reflects this larger picture of capital mobility. Granted, competition with southern markets was keen. But if Penobscot had diversified into further processing products or had developed an aggressive advertising campaign in the 1970s, might the story have unfolded differently? Linda spoke on several occasions about the plant's obsolete machinery, and in her narrative she discussed how poorly it was maintained. Why did the Lewises fail to reinvest (or reinvest too late) in order to bring the plant up to date?[78] Penobscot's owner, Bernard Lewis, stated that he was "ordered" by the family to liquidate the business; he also insisted that the cost of upgrading would have equaled the losses they had already seen: $5 million.[79] One wonders why the company didn't recognize the changing structure of the industry *earlier*. Might Penobscot have survived if the company had responded more rapidly to market forces and made the significant investments necessary to stay current and competitive with the national market? Or what if Penobscot and the state's other processors had invested in an improved rail transport system?[80] When Maplewood filed for bankruptcy in 1979, some critics said that the owners had not reinvested adequately in the company and instead had siphoned off too much of the profits.[81] William Bell, executive director of the Maine Poultry Federation, a trade association formed by the processing companies, called such claims "patently untrue."[82] But was Penobscot simply a losing proposition, as the poultry interests would have us believe? Or did the Lewis family liquidate the business in order to invest elsewhere, in something more profitable?

Since Penobscot's corporate records are not in the public domain, we may never know precisely what happened to Penobscot Poultry. However, some of the circumstances surrounding the decline of the industry and the Lewis family's other holdings provide potential clues. In 1981, the *Maine Times* argued that the decline of poultry "was not so much a collapse as it was an exodus from the state." Of the five broiler-processing companies that dominated Maine's industry, only Maplewood went completely out of business. Penobscot was still thriving "with the help of other commercial ventures." The remaining three firms, Lipman Poultry Co., Fort Halifax Poultry Co., and Hillcrest Foods, Inc., "*continue[d] to have poultry or other operations in other states*" [my emphasis].[83] According to a January 1980 *Bangor Daily News* article, Hillcrest had been "forced" to open a poultry operation in the South six months earlier, ostensibly because of high production costs in Maine. The Hillcrest spokesperson refused to disclose the new plant's location or its impact on Hillcrest's Maine operation, but by May 1981, the Maine-based plant was shut down.[84] The implication here is capital migration; the decline of the industry fits the generalized pattern of businesses relocating to regions that offer a better "business climate."[85]

As for Penobscot Poultry, we can only surmise as to the nature of the "other commercial ventures" that enabled Penobscot to outlive Lipman, Fort Halifax, and Hillcrest. In 1981, Lewis sold a number of his Portland properties and purchased Maplewood (then in receivership) for $1 million.[86] The *Maine Times* noted that "there are reports that George Lewis, owner of the only operating poultry-processing plant in Maine and *who has poultry firms in two other states*, may well take over the entire Maine industry" [emphasis mine].[87] George Lewis's obituary, which noted the companies he had owned in his lifetime, made no mention of any out-of-state poultry firms and whether they were still in operation upon his death in 1987.[88] However, we do know that upon Bernard Lewis's death in 1989, although Penobscot *as a firm* may not have survived, "the company's holdings ha[d] gone into the Cross Street Realty Trust," which is managed by Lewis's brother David, also a Portland resident.[89]

Linda Lord and others familiar with Maine's poultry industry have commented that one of the fundamental reasons for Penobscot's closing was that the younger generation of Lewises had no real interest or key motivation in pursuing the poultry-processing business.[90] George Lewis had grown up in a family tradition of meat processing. Although Bernard shared his father's passion for the industry, meat processing seemed to play a somewhat less central role in his career.[91] Bernard's children, as Linda and others have suggested, may have been yet another step removed from the family legacy, so that the motivation to reinvest in Penobscot simply may not have been there—especially if other family business ventures offered more immediate short-term gains.

Whatever the contributing factors, the fact remains that Maine's poultry-processing industry did not survive. While the broiler processor owners may have transferred their holdings to other firms, what transpired for the workers? What did Penobscot's closing—indeed, what does a shutdown of any significant industry in a region—mean for workers like Linda Lord?

To date, we have little hard data about the social costs of deindustrialization to both men and women, but the existing studies show these costs to be considerable. At a minimum, a plant shutdown produces short-term unemployment. Workers not only lose their jobs; often, the subsequent jobs they find do not provide comparable income or benefits.[92] Having lost their seniority, they are also vulnerable to layoffs on their new jobs. These consequences are especially severe during a recession and for towns or regions where there are few employment opportunities. Studies reveal that at least one-third of those affected by a plant closing will experience long-term unemployment.[93] Women are twice as likely to be found unemployed a year after job loss.[94] Displaced older workers also encounter long periods of unemployment and declines in earnings trajectories.[95] Minorities are particularly vulnerable because of their concentration in urban centers where plant closings have been most prominent.[96]

But the incidence of job loss, the duration of unemployment, and impaired job stability are only a few of the personal costs associated with plant closings. Often workers and their families end up totally depleting their savings and may even be forced to sell their homes to avoid foreclosure.[97] Physical and mental health can also be adversely affected. Illnesses related to stress are particularly common, as well as high rates of depression and increased numbers of suicide. Families and communities suffer as well; studies of the effects of mass unemployment, for instance, point to increased crime and violence in the affected community.[98] One of the chief concerns expressed by workers who have survived plant closings, however, is the loss of health benefits. Depending on whether a firm liquidates or goes bankrupt, workers can often be left with no coverage whatsoever.[99]

Linda's experience after Penobscot's closing keenly illustrates the effects of industrial decline on women workers. First, the job retraining course—frequently touted

Lunchroom at Penobscot Poultry. February 1988.

as a means by which workers can start anew—did not enable Linda to retool easily for the postindustrial age. Because she had been blinded in one eye on the job, she was ill equipped to maintain the reading load required for the oil furnace course she had enrolled in. Perhaps equally discouraging was the experience of being shoved aside, literally, by the men in the class as all the students gathered around the oil burner for instruction. Linda dropped out of the course and continued her job search. But she felt hampered in the process not only by her difficulties with the job retraining course but also by her lack of higher education. As she said of her oldest brother, "He's got the education behind him, so he can probably step out and get another good job somewhere." Her brother's master's degree enabled him to retool and gain employment far more quickly than his sister.[100]

It should be noted that in other ways, however, Linda defied the statistics; in that sense, her experience may have been the exception rather than the rule. Within six months of losing her job, she found work at a local ropemaking factory employing 30–35 workers. Linda feels that she has improved her work situation, despite the job's insecurity. The work is a lot cleaner, and she gets a better hourly wage, although she is paid per piece. As she puts it, "Well, I tell you, looking at ten miles of rope goes a lot faster than watching chickens go by on a line." She considers herself fortunate to have found work in one of the few remaining industries in the area. Although she has solid medical coverage, she has no retirement benefits. With cuts in the defense industry and the resultant layoffs, job security and her long-term economic stability remain uncertain.

Linda—like many displaced workers—did not opt for the solution most frequently suggested for those who can no longer make a living in a deindustrialized area. Studies have shown that while most people migrate for economic reasons, workers with jobs will rarely sacrifice them to move to another region that offers higher wages. The economic costs of a move are only one of many concerns. The psychological costs, the loss of friendship and community ties associated with migration, cannot be easily measured.[101] And migration is not always a viable option. Families headed by workers in midcareer often have financial obligations that keep them from relocating and taking just "any job" at less pay.[102] Women—single parents especially—cannot easily pick up and move to another area in search of work. Women who are charged with the responsibility for an aging or infirm parent—as they often are in our society—likewise are restricted in their mobility. "And one cannot move a parent who has grown up, lived, and looks forward, in fact, to dying in a place. A society cannot demand that that person leave," as historian Paula Petrik comments.[103] Linda Lord wanted to stay in the Belfast area not only because Brooks was her home but also because she needed—and wanted—to tend to her aging parents.

But we cannot evaluate Linda's experience strictly within the confines of her own individual goals and interests and her position within the family structure, a point made by Tom Dublin in his book, *Transforming Women's Work*.[104] Linda's community was absolutely central in her decision to remain in the area after Penobscot closed. She has served on the volunteer fire department in Brooks for over twenty-five years and has been an ambulance attendant for over ten years, the career she says she would have pursued had she furthered her education. She continues to help out friends and community members, whether it be a local restaurateur who is having troubles with his heating system or a friend who needs help hand-slaughtering chickens. Over the past twenty years, Linda has played drums for local country western music bands; the group with whom she currently plays, the Frye Mountain Band, already has gigs lined up for the summer. And summertime will also enable her to bring out both her motorcycle and her "trike" (her three-wheeled motorcycle, one of her newer acquisitions). Linda loves to hunt and fish, and she likes living in the country with her dogs. All of these aspects of Linda's life—not simply her role as family caretaker—keep her wedded, perhaps in the truest sense of the word, to her home community of Brooks, Maine. As Laurel Thatcher Ulrich has noted, "Neighborliness, in all of its ramifications, is one of the most important and neglected aspects of female history in early America."[105] When we examine the role of community in the lives of women like Linda Lord, we see all the more clearly why women in the midst of industrial decline are unlikely to uproot themselves from their homes and communities to seek out ostensibly better jobs elsewhere. We can also begin to see the range of factors—gender, rural values, class, and family dynamics—influencing Linda's experience, both before and after the plant's closing.

Beyond the experience of the individual, there are also the "ripple effects" within the community. Employees lose salaries, pensions, and fringe benefits; suppliers lose their contracts; and government agencies at all levels lose corporate and personal income tax revenue, as well as commercial property tax revenue. The economic effects can be devastating to an area. When a "company town" loses its primary employer, the effects are only magnified.[106] According to the U.S. Department of Labor, when one manufacturing job is lost in Maine, an additional one and one-third jobs are lost in the state as a whole.[107] The public sector suffers losses as well. When a plant closes, federal, state, and local tax revenues decrease and social expenditures increase. But costs at the local level can often be most devastating. When General Motors closed its assembly plant in Norwood, Ohio, in 1987, over 40 percent of Norwood's jobs were lost. Beyond income loss to Norwood residents and businesses, the city of Norwood also lost $2.6 million per year in earnings taxes from GM workers. To recoup the loss, the city levied an $8 million tax on city residents.[108] In essence, the residents had "paid" for the closing through the loss of their jobs and income *and* through increased taxes. When companies pull their capital out of a region, then, local communities are essentially left holding the bag. Linda herself states the importance of industries' support of the tax base: "I'd like to see more industries in and around. It helps on your taxes, and it keeps the store owners happy."[109]

It is here that we return to the issue of community versus capital.[110] What *do* businesses owe to the communities in which they operate? One answer can be drawn from the case of the Youngstown shutdown in 1979, when a group of union representatives and lawyers filed suit against U.S. Steel to prevent it from closing the mills. During the proceedings, the presiding judge speculated aloud regarding a community's right to recompense for its years of service:

> It seems to me that a property right has arisen from this lengthy, long-established relationship between United States Steel, the steel industry as an institution, the community in Youngstown, the people in Mahoning County, and the Mahoning Valley in having given and devoted their lives to this industry. Perhaps not a property right to the extent that can be remedied by compelling U.S. Steel to remain in Youngstown. I think the law could not possibly recognize that type of an obligation. But I think the law can recognize the property right to the extent that U.S. Steel cannot leave that Mahoning Valley and the Youngstown area in a state of waste, that it cannot completely abandon its obligation to that community, because certain vested rights have arisen out of this long relationship and institution.[111]

Ultimately, the judge could determine no legal basis for the finding of a property right and hence dismissed the claim. No precedent had yet been set.[112] His effort to grapple with this issue, however, raised key points in support of a community's claim to reparations.

In other cases, efforts to hold corporations accountable have proved more successful. Duluth, Minnesota, for instance, won a lawsuit against a firm that used a $10 million Industrial Development Revenue Bond to secure a low-interest loan to purchase the Diamond Tool and Horseshoe Company. The conglomerate that bought the company shifted work out of the area, although the purpose of the subsidy had been to enable Diamond Tool—Duluth's largest employer—to stay open.[113] Corporate accountability, many argue, can only be secured through creating long-term and far-reaching national industrial development policies that serve to protect workers' pay

Linda backing a truck into the Brooks Volunteer Fire Department building. April 1988.

and rights.[114] Others argue that protection of U.S. workers will only be achieved through legislation that seeks to eliminate the tax advantages that encourage corporations to restructure through acquisitions, mergers, and capital mobility at the expense of U.S. jobs and workers.[115] Linda Lord likewise implies that government should take a more active role in keeping U.S. industry from abandoning communities: "I think way back they [meaning both the U.S. government and the corporations] should have been looking out more for the American people." They should have been "try[ing] to keep business right here."[116] Economist William Greider argues for a "one world" market that attempts to redress economic imbalances of supply and demand across the globe.[117]

Linda Lord's comment reinforces economist Barry Bluestone's assessment: "What deindustrialization ignores is that 'people want to improve their community, not abdicate from it.'"[118] How, then, can individuals who choose *not* to abdicate revitalize their communities? Richard Barringer suggests, "In such a world of competition, productivity means everything. The ability to get as much as possible out of a single dollar of investment, a single investment of any element of human labor. That requires capital, its investment, and its reinvestment in this community itself."[119] Bluestone describes an assessment of community resources and needs that was successfully carried out for southeastern Michigan—strategies that could be used elsewhere and that could be especially important to places like Maine.[120] More grassroots efforts include the example of Ivanhoe, Virginia, in which the community responded to the mine closings by building its own local revitalization programs.[121] Such local efforts may ultimately prove most successful either in slowing down the flight of capital or in responding creatively to a town's circumstances after the industry leaves.

To its credit, Maine boasts the nation's most progressive legislation on plant closings. It requires advance notification and one week's severance pay for every year of seniority with the plant.[122] Yet a recent study of Maine plant closings from 1971 (when legislation was first enacted) to 1982 demonstrates that the efficacy of the law has been hampered by the confidentiality of notification, the lack of penalties for failure to provide notice, and the low level of compliance with the regulations.[123] Maine's law was recently challenged—but upheld—in federal court. In 1987, it was reviewed before the U.S. Supreme Court and sustained; it may well set an important precedent for states' abilities to restrict capital mobility.[124]

Another promising development is that Maine's leaders seem to be taking a more active role in deterring capital flight. When the Warnaco Group announced it would sell or close its Waterville, Maine, division of Hathaway, the nation's oldest shirtmaker, Governor Angus King began actively searching for a buyer.[125]

In the meantime, Maine's economy—with lumbering and fishing now in decline—depends heavily on tourism. Linda Lord and Carolyn Chute both see this as a stop-gap measure. In her narrative, Linda discusses the recent efforts to turn Belfast into a "tourist place," and she says, in her usual clipped, incisive manner: "It will not work. You can't get enough tourist people coming in. And why should they hit Belfast when there's a lot prettier sights around in the state of Maine?"

Regardless of the strategies Maine and other states could and should undertake to support their communities, the fundamental issue—the struggle—remains the same. We are all faced with this dilemma: under what conditions does our economic system undermine our efforts to create healthy and stable communities? Is there a balance to be found between the "needs" of capital and the needs of those of us who build and sustain communities? How can we negotiate with corporations and conglomerates, when their goal is profit, regardless of what that profit costs on a local level?

The irony, of course, is that many of us reap the benefits of our capital-driven system. On the one hand, we drive our imported automobiles and buy low-cost items at K-Mart, made in Asia or Latin America by underpaid nonunion workers. On the other hand, we pay dearly when our plants relocate to a more "business-friendly" environment. Like Linda, it would seem that we are content and not content with our predicament, struggling to balance our needs and desires with the limitations—or what appear to be the limitations—of our circumstances. Yet ultimately our political system is what we have chosen—or at least abided. Our internal conflict over the choice—the balancing act of capital versus community—may in fact reflect a kind of divided consciousness. We know our predicament, and we do comply, albeit reluctantly. But as environmentalist Rachel Carson asked in *Silent Spring*, "Have we fallen into a mesmerized state that makes us accept as inevitable that which is inferior or detrimental, as though having lost the will or the vision to demand that which is good?"[126] And so we must ask ourselves: What did it cost Linda Lord and others like her when Penobscot closed its doors? What does it cost us all when our local businesses flee? And when is the cost too high?

Notes

1. Barry Bluestone, "Deindustrialization and Unemployment in America," *Deindustrialization and Plant Closure*, ed. Paul D. Staudohar and Holly E. Brown (Lexington, Mass.: D.C. Heath, 1987) 8. See also Barry Bluestone and Bennett Harrison, *The Deindustrialization of America: Plant Closings, Community Abandonment, and the Dismantling of Basic Industry* (New York: Basic Books, 1982).

2. Donald Bartlett and James Steele, *America: What Went Wrong?* (Kansas City: Andrews and McMeel, 1992) 18.

3. "Downsizing in America," *New York Times*, 3–9 March 1996. It remains to be seen whether the 1993 passage of the North American Free Trade Agreement (NAFTA) and the most recent round of amendments to the General Agreement on Tariffs and Trade (GATT) will lead to further decline in U.S. industries and jobs, as critics have predicted.

4. Jay Davis, "Chicken Big: A Journalist's Perspective," lecture delivered at the project's original exhibit opening, Belfast Free Library, Belfast, Maine, 23 February 1989.

5. Barry Bluestone, "In Support of the Deindustrialization Thesis," *Deindustrialization and Plant Closure*, ed. Staudohar and Brown, 44.

6. Richard E. Barringer, "An Economic Perspective on Waldo County," lecture delivered at the project's original exhibit opening, Belfast Free Library, Belfast, Maine, 23 February 1989.

7. Frank E. Claes, Introduction to *Waldo County: The Way It Was* (Camden, Maine: Down East Books, 1985) vii–viii.

8. James S. Leamon, "Maine in the American Revolution, 1763–1787," in *Maine: The Pine Tree State from Prehistory to the Present*, ed. Richard W. Judd, Edwin A. Churchill, and Joel W. Eastman (Orono: University of Maine Press, 1995) 145. See also Samuel Waldo, *A Defence of the Title of the late John Leverett Esq; to a Tract of Land in the Eastern Parts of the Province of the Massachusetts Bay, commonly called Muscongus Lands, lying upon St. George's Muscongus and Penobscott Rivers* (Boston, 1736), typescript copy in the Samuel Waldo Papers, Maine Historical Society, Collection 34, box 1, folder 5A, pp. 3.1–3, 4.1–3.

9. Joel W. Eastman, *A History of Sears Island, Searsport, Maine* (Searsport: Searsport Historical Society, 1976) 15–17. See also William D. Williamson, *The History of the State of Maine; From Its First Discovery, A.D. 1602, to the Separation, A.D. 1820, Inclusive*, vol. 2 (Hallowell, Maine: Glazier, Masters, and Smith, 1839) 238, 335–38, 455. For a biographical sketch of Samuel Waldo, see Waldo Lincoln, comp., *Genealogy of the Waldo Family: A Record of the Descendants of Cornelius Waldo of Ipswich, Mass., from 1642 to 1900*, vol. 1 (Worcester, Mass.: Press of Charles Hamilton, 1902) 96–105.

10. Joseph Williamson, *The History of the City of Belfast, Maine*, vol. 1 (1877; Somersworth, N.H.: New England History Press, 1982) 677–79.

11. Richard E. Barringer, "Waldo County: Historical Profile," unpublished manuscript, 2–3. See also Barringer lecture.

12. Lang 46.

13. Barringer, "Waldo County," 3. J. D. B. DeBow, *The Seventh Census of the United States: 1850* (Washington, D.C.: Robert Armstrong, 1853).

14. Barringer lecture.

15. Richard F. Saunders, *Contract Broiler Growing in Maine*, Maine Agricultural Experiment Station, bulletin 571 (Orono: University of Maine, May 1958) 7.

16. "The Maine Broiler," *New England Business Review*, June 1961: 1.

17. Barringer, "Waldo County," 6.

18. Barringer lecture. For an illuminating discussion of women's roles in southern poultry production, see Lu Ann Jones, "Re-visioning the Countryside: Southern Women, Rural Reform, and the Farm Economy in the Twentieth Century," Ph.D. diss., University of North Carolina–Chapel Hill, 1996. See esp. chap. 4, "'So I Went into the Chicken Business': Southern Farm Women and Poultry Production," 110–47. Jones argues that during the first four decades of the twentieth century, southern farm women often turned to poultry as a sideline for securing additional farm income, at a time when the raising of poultry was considered "women's work." These women took advantage of a growing market for fowl and eggs, adopting new production methods, and participated in marketing to advance their farm's poultry enterprises. In the process, southern farm women helped prove the profitability of poultry and paved the way for the agribusiness that took off in the 1940s. A comparable close-grained study of women and poultry production in the Northeast, which is beyond the scope of this current study, might well yield similar findings.

19. Lynne Langley, "The Lipmans: Big Chicken and Egg Men from Augusta," *Maine Times*, 24 September 1971: 2.

20. Oscar A. Hanke, John L. Skinner, and James H. Florea, eds., *American Poultry History, 1823–1973* (Madison, Wisc.: American Poultry Historical Society, 1974) 418. See also Bernard Lewis, lecture delivered at the project's original exhibit opening, Belfast Free Library, Belfast, Maine, 23 February 1989.

21. Davis lecture.

22. Langley, "The Lipmans," 2. See also Frank D. Reed, *The Maine Poultry Industry: Its Impact, Growth, and Competitive Position*, Cooperative Extension Service, circular 394 (Orono: University of Maine, July 1970) 2–3.

23. Hanke 420, 558–60. See also Reed 2–3; Gordon Sawyer, *The Agribusiness Poultry Industry: A History of Its Development* (New York: Exposition Press, 1971) 72–84; "The Maine Broiler" 2; and "$10 Million Boost in Maine's No. 1 Farm Product Seen," *Portland Sunday Telegram*, 4 December 1955: 1A.

24. Hanke 420, 560.

25. Lewis lecture. See also Hanke 421–23.

26. Hanke 771. "Waldo County: An Area Where Industry, Agriculture, Recreational Industries Compliment Each Other," *Maine Sunday Telegram*, 4 March 1973: n.p.

27. Hanke 426–28; Barringer, "Waldo County," 6.

28. For an illuminating example of the industry's and the community's perceptions of the poultry business, see G. E. Coleman Jr., "Broiler Day," *Maine Poultry Improvement Association* (Belfast, Maine: Journal Press, 1949) 47, 49.

29. Barringer, "Waldo County," 6. See also Bill Caldwell, "Belfast's Battle of Chicken Guts," *Maine Sunday Telegram*, 12 September 1971: 9D.

30. "George I. Lewis, 83, Philanthropist, Dies," *Portland Press Herald*, 16 May 1987: 37.

31. Lewis lecture. It should be noted that Penobscot Poultry Co., Inc., was formally known as Poultry Processing, Inc. Research conducted through the State of Maine Bureau of Corporations, Elections and Commissions turned up a long history of name changes, mergers, and other legal transactions surrounding the company. In his lecture, Lewis cites Penobscot's start date as 1949 under Al Savitz, when Savitz first did "New York dressed" poultry. The earliest articles of incorporation, though, can be dated to 1905 (Penobscot Poultry Company in Bucksport, Maine). That company ceased transactions in 1906. In 1945, MacLeod Poultry Co. filed articles of incorporation in Belfast. In 1951, the name changed to Penobscot Poultry Co., Inc., and in 1963 the name changed again to Waldo Enterprises, Inc. Evidently that company ceased operations (or was "excused") in 1964. Poultry Processing, Inc., first filed articles of incorporation in 1965. Lewis stated in his lecture that Savitz, with Lewis backing, bought back the company from Corn Products Company (later CPC International, legally known as Best Foods) right around that time. Poultry Processing, Inc., remained in legal standing at the Bureau of Corporations through 1994. Articles of incorporation were filed *again* in 1994 (Penobscot Poultry Company, Inc., in Bangor, Maine) but ceased once again in 1995. Poultry Processing, Inc., evidently claimed the name of Penobscot Poultry throughout its tenure in Belfast. I use here the legal name of Penobscot Poultry Co., Inc. (and Penobscot Poultry, as it was known locally), because that is ostensibly the company Savitz "started" and the Lewises took over upon Savitz's death. See Bureau of Corporations card files, vol. 52, p. 379; vol. 127, p. 112.

32. "Chickens: Skimming the Fat," *Maine Times*, 2 June 1972: 4.

33. "Gov't Files Suit Against Belfast Poultry Firm," *Maine Sunday Telegram*, 31 October 1971: 19A.

34. "More Maine Poultry Found Contaminated," *Portland Press Herald*, 1 March 1972: 24.

35. "Chickens: Cheapest Ever," *Maine Times*, 17 March 1972: 5. See also "PCB and the Chickens," *Maine Times*, 31 March 1972: 23.

36. Lynne Langley, "Gassing the Chickens: It Could Be Disaster for the Farmer," *Maine Times*, 3 March 1972: 7.

37. Bill Caldwell, "Censors Remove Meat from Maine Poultry Report," *Maine Sunday Telegram*, 4 March 1973: 5A.

38. Barringer, "Waldo County," 7; Denise Bailey, "The Great Poultry Failure," *Maine Times*, 17 July 1981: 4.

39. Lewis lecture.

40. For a discussion of the Maine poultry industry and its competition with southern markets, see Christian T. Cartter, *The U.S. Broiler Boom: New Pressures and New Possibilities for Maine's Contract Poultry Growers* (Bath, Maine: Coastal Enterprises, 1980) 2–18. In 1981, David Shaw Associates analyzed cost differentials between Maine broiler firms and twenty-five eastern companies (including the Delmarva

region and the South), including labor rates. Maine averaged $5.75/hour with benefits; the twenty-five eastern companies (as a composite) averaged $4.65/hour with benefits. Broiler processor wages in the South were typically lower than those in the Delmarva region. Maine processing labor costs amounted to one cent per pound over the average for the twenty-five eastern companies. Shaw also points out that a high degree of automation in newer plants typically improves productivity and, despite higher wages, may result in lower costs per pound of chicken (17–18). For a discussion of how the South has historically lured industry by suppressing wages and conditions, see James C. Cobb, *The Selling of the South: The Southern Crusade for Industrial Development, 1936–1980* (Baton Rouge: Louisiana State University Press, 1982).

41. Bailey 3.

42. Denise Goodman, "Belfast Now and Tomorrow," *Maine Times*, 18 July 1980: 3.

43. Bluestone and Harrison 6–7. For a recent example, see also Sara Rimer, "Fall of a Shirtmaking Legend Shakes Its Maine Hometown," *New York Times*, 15 May 1996: A1, A13. On 6 May 1996, the Warnaco Group announced it would sell or close its Waterville division of Hathaway, the nation's oldest shirtmaker, despite the fact that the company had recently doubled its productivity. The workers—95 percent of whom are women—had forfeited their raises, among other strategies, in an effort to keep the factory open. Linda J. Wachner, the chief executive, stated the Waterville division would be closed because it "wasn't making money" (A13). Her company—whose holdings include major clothing lines such as Calvin Klein and Ralph Lauren—netted $46.5 million in 1995. Wachner's salary that year totaled $10 million in salary and stock. For a more detailed discussion of capital mobility and forms of disinvestment, see Bluestone and Harrison 140–90.

44. Hanke 382–87.

45. Bailey 3.

46. Bailey 5.

47. David Shaw Associates, *An Analysis of the Economic Viability of the Maine Broiler Industry* (Augusta, Maine: Maller Development Services, 1981) 35–36, 44–45.

48. Hanke 428, citing Ray Cook, "Broilers: Billion-Dollar Business," *N.H. Breeder and Broiler Grower* 17.1 (January 1954).

49. Eunice T. Cox, "New Man, New Approach: Stewart Smith Exudes Optimism About the Future of Maine Farming," *Maine Times*, 4 January 1980: 3.

50. Hanke 430.

51. It should be noted that in 1976 Hillcrest Foods, Inc., in Lewiston, Maine, came out with a chicken called "Pure One," using an air-chilled versus water-chilled cooling system. But the company's effort at brand name recognition did not pan out. David Shaw commented that "not every attempt to establish [brand name] products will work. . . . The trade has to be right. It takes a tremendous effort, lots of money and advertising" (Bailey 5–6). Some poultry producers were well aware of the steps necessary to remain nationally competitive. In his remarks at the 1983 Maine Poultry Conference, Bernard Lewis predicted that "within two years branded [chicken sold by brand name] poultry will dominate the marketplace in the U.S.A." He noted further that Valmac and Tyson were emerging as the dominant forces in the food service market. He also commented, "In the plant, higher line speeds, combined with better equipment and new methods, will keep the competition keen—but only for those with courage to spend money in large quantities and as rapidly as possible. . . . We need imagination, courage, a deep pocketbook, and a strong will to survive." See "The Outlook for Broilers," *Poultry Newsletter*, Cooperative Extension Service (Orono: University of Maine, 1983) 6–7. According to Linda Lord, George Lewis had talked about switching over to further processing, but after his death those plans never materialized (personal communication, 5 January 1997).

52. David Shaw Associates 24.

53. Bailey 3–4.

54. David Shaw Associates 51–54.

55. Langley, "The Lipmans," 3.

56. "Poultry: Grain Price," *Maine Times*, 7 May 1971: 11.

57. Cox 3.

58. David Shaw Associates 53. It should be noted that in late 1979 through 1983, concerted efforts were made to save the state's failing poultry-processing industry. Poultry growers banded together initially in an effort to form a cooperative and buy out Maplewood, but these early organizing efforts failed. Industry leaders and state officials, such as William Bell, executive director of the Maine Poultry Federation, and State Agricultural Commissioner Stewart Smith, proved instrumental in helping to orga-

nize growers over the next few years. Growers formed the Committee to Save Maine Poultry and later the Maine Pride Poultry Cooperative, which eventually tried to reopen Hillcrest Foods, Inc., in Lewiston. Meanwhile, Governor Joseph Brennan and other state leaders lobbied for a $3 million bond to build the much sought-after feed grain terminal, and undertook additional strategies to save the industry. But when the Maine Poultry Federation negotiated a reduction in rail costs, it was later determined that the $3 million bond should go instead to support a cargo port at Sears Island. One wonders if the terminal had been built whether the story of Maine's processing industry might have unfolded differently. Or perhaps, at this late date, these well-intentioned efforts were simply too late in coming. By all signs, poultry processing was already deep in trouble. See David Bright, "Growers Form Maplewood Plan," *Bangor Daily News*, 31 December 1979: 18; "Poultrymen Pessimistic About Plans for Co-op," *Portland Press Herald*, 13 March 1981: 1, 8; Elizabeth H. Holland, "Chicken Farmers Dig In to Help Ailing Industry," *Portland Press Herald*, 13 March 1981: 28; William T. Murphy, "Bonds May Revive State Poultry Farms," *Bangor Daily News*, 9 November 1981: 1; "Hillcrest Selected by Co-op," *Bangor Daily News*, 19 October 1981: 21; "Grain Terminal: Poultry Growers Hesitate," *Maine Times*, 27 November 1981: 10.

59. Bailey 3–4. See also Kenneth E. Wing and Wilbert C. Geiss Jr., *Estimated Cash Flows and Profitability of Maine Broiler Farms*, Life Sciences and Agriculture Experiment Station, Bulletin 694 (Orono: University of Maine, December 1971). This study not only points out the industry's dependence on FmHA loans but also notes that FmHA policies had not kept pace with the industry's technological changes. There were two major problems with the FmHA loan policies: (1) FmHA would lend on a maximum size of thirty thousand square feet of building, yet the maximum efficiency for producing birds was forty thousand square feet; and (2) most loans were financed on a twenty-five- to forty-year program, when in fact most buildings would become obsolete after fifteen years, requiring the producer to finance a new operation with debt still outstanding on the original investment, or cease operations at that point and pay the debt through other means. The study recommended that the size of the broiler operation must increase, the contract rates must increase, or the interest rates must decrease, in order for the farm operator to accumulate capital for future investment. Unless these changes occurred, "additional investment in broiler housing by the processors will be necessary to maintain the position of the Maine broiler industry" (36–37).

60. Lloyd Ferris, "Doom and Gloom in Chicken Glut Creek," *Maine Sunday Telegram*, 30 January 1972: 1D, 5D. Earlier research in genetics may have helped set the stage for overproduction in the industry. For the impact of genetics research on improved poultry production, see "The Maine Broiler" 2–3.

61. Barringer, "Waldo County," 8. See C. Hasty Thompson, "Costs Up, Prices Down," *Maine Sunday Telegram*, 19 August 1979. See also Bailey 3.

62. Barringer, "Waldo County," 9. See also U.S. Department of Commerce, Bureau of Economic Analysis, *Regional Information System, 1969–1996*, CD published May 1998.

63. *The Maine Economy: Year-End Review and Outlook* (Augusta: Maine State Planning Office, December 1995) 13.

64. Barringer lecture. This was especially true of poultry without product differentiation and diversification.

65. Nancy R. Folbre, Julia L. Leighton, and Melissa R. Roderick, "Legislation in Maine," *Deindustrialization and Plant Closure*, ed. Staudohar and Brown, 293.

66. During this period, it is important to note that manufacturing grew slowly in comparison with the service sector. From 1971 to 1981, manufacturing jobs increased by 12 percent, while the service sector showed an increase of 72 percent. See *County Business Patterns 1971, Maine* (Washington, D.C.: GPO, 1972) and *County Business Patterns 1981, Maine* (Washington, D.C.: GPO, 1982). Over this period, per capita income in Waldo County declined from 86 percent of the state average to less than 81 percent of the state average. In essence, the county lost ground, in part because of poultry's decline. See U.S. Department of Commerce, Bureau of Economic Analysis, *Regional Economic Information System, 1969–1996*, CD published May 1998.

67. Folbre, Leighton, and Roderick 297. For a discussion of bankruptcy and its links to deindustrialization, see also Bartlett and Steele 66–68. The authors argue that congressional streamlining of the Bankruptcy Code in 1978 actually made bankruptcy easier for troubled businesses. This shift, in combination with substantial corporate borrowing and leveraged buyouts in the 1980s, led to four times as many bankruptcy petitions in the 1980s as compared with the 1960s.

68. Harry Browne and Beth Sims, *Runaway America: U.S. Jobs and Factories on the Move* (Albuquerque: Resource Center, 1993) 62.

69. Bluestone and Harrison 6.

70. Browne and Sims 16, 18.

71. Ronald Kwan, "Footloose and Country Free: Mobility Key to Capitalists' Power," *Dollars and Sense*, March 1991: 7.

72. Browne and Sims 21–22.

73. Bluestone and Harrison 8.

74. Bluestone and Harrison 15–19.

75. Bluestone and Harrison 6–7; for a more detailed discussion of capital mobility and forms of disinvestment, see also Bluestone and Harrison 140–90.

76. Browne and Sims 10. For a discussion of the restructuring of U.S. corporations through acquisitions, mergers, and speculative investments, and the impact on American workers, see Bartlett and Steele, *America: What Went Wrong?*

77. Michael Wallace and Joyce Rothschild, "Plant Closings, Capital Flight, and Worker Dislocation: The Long Shadow of Deindustrialization," *Deindustrialization and the Restructuring of American Industry*, Research in Politics and Society, vol. 3, ed. Michael Wallace and Joyce Rothschild (Greenwich, Conn.: JAI Press, 1988) 7–8.

78. It is interesting to note here that Al Savitz had converted to evisceration only in 1955, which was late in comparison with other plants nationwide.

79. Lewis lecture.

80. One of the underlying problems with the industry seemed to be a fundamental lack of willingness to compete—that is, to change strategies for competition continually in the face of a changing market. For instance, a number of sources acknowledged that the fierce competition among the state's poultry producers often interfered with their efforts to work together to solve the industry's fundamental ills. In 1973, Herbert Hutchings, general manager at Penobscot Poultry, argued that "we will not get anywhere in Maine unless processor and grower get together on problems, such as freight rate." He noted that, as an industry, they were a minority [as opposed to the nation] and needed the leverage they could gain through cooperative efforts: "Our life is in jeopardy unless we get together." See Herbert Hutchings, "The Maine Broiler Processors—and What They Are Doing to Keep the Maine Broiler Industry Competitive," *Maine Poultry Improvement Association Yearbook 1973* (Belfast, Maine: Journal Press, 1973) 15, 17. In this instance, cooperation was the best strategy for competition on the national level. This "willingness to compete" would have meant sometimes pursuing strategies that were different or in some way challenging to the status quo.

81. Goodman 3. Economist Michael Montagna has suggested that businesses owned and managed by families are often more reluctant to take capital risks than corporate-owned companies; they are less likely to seek investors, go into debt, or leverage a family fortune in order to build their businesses (personal communication, 7 January 1997). David A. Carlton and Peter A. Coclanis make a similar argument about small southern textile companies dependent on small investors; see Carlton and Coclanis, "Capital Mobilization and Southern Industry, 1880–1905: The Case of the Carolina Piedmont," in *Journal of Economic History* 49 (March 1989): 73–94.

82. Bailey 3.

83. Bailey 3.

84. Dennis O. Brown, "Poultry Firm Is 'Forced' to Expand in Southland," *Bangor Daily News*, 17 January 1980: 23.

85. This term usually implies an environment that offers low-wage and nonunionized labor, as well as generous tax incentives, to attract businesses.

86. Frank Sleeper, "Lewis Acquires Poultry Company," *Portland Evening Express*, 13 February 1981: 11.

87. Bailey 3.

88. "George I. Lewis, 83, Philanthropist, Dies" 37. The implication here is that if Lewis's other poultry firms were viable operations when Penobscot closed, the family may have reinvested in their out-of-state poultry businesses. Often industries will set up parallel plants in different locations and then downsize or close one firm while investing in the other (which would seem to be the case with Hillcrest). If this were true for Penobscot, its closing would likewise fit the prevailing pattern of capital flight. But again, without access to company records, such a case is virtually impossible to prove.

89. Tom Groening, "Lewis Willing to Talk About Poultry Plant," *Republican Journal*, 4 August 1994: A1.

90. Author's personal communication with Linda Lord, 7 August 1994; personal communication with Belfast journalist Jay Davis, 8 August 1994; personal communication with Dr. Harris (Animal and Veterinary Sciences, University of Maine), 2 April 1993.

91. Lewis lecture; see also "Bernard J. Lewis, Prominent Maine Businessman," *Portland Press Herald*, 30 May 1989: 35.

92. Wallace and Rothschild 19–20.

93. Bluestone and Harrison 51–53.

94. Bluestone and Harrison 54.

95. Folbre, Leighton, and Roderick 294. Some argue that older workers, though clearly hard hit by plant closings, are often past their years of greatest financial pressures (i.e., paying off home mortgages, etc.) and may not be as hard hit as middle-aged employees. See Carrie R. Leana and Daniel C. Feldman, "The Psychology of Job Loss," *Research in Personnel and Human Resources Management* 12 (1994): 284.

96. Bluestone and Harrison 54–55.

97. Bluestone and Harrison 63–72.

98. Wallace and Rothschild 22–24.

99. Bartlett and Steele 130–34.

100. In a recent conversation with Linda (13 May 1996), I learned that Linda's brother was not the only family member to receive higher education. Her sister also attended college, earned a teaching certificate, and then taught in Hartford, Connecticut, before returning to the Portland area. Linda mentioned in her oral history that right after high school she (Linda) went into the hospital for an operation and was not supposed to work for a year; whether this affected her possibilities for further schooling is unclear. We have never pressed Linda on this particular point.

101. Bluestone and Harrison 99–103.

102. Wallace and Rothschild 24.

103. Paula Petrik, "Walking the Line: Women in Industrial Labor," lecture delivered at the project's original exhibit opening, Belfast Free Library, Belfast, Maine, 23 February 1989, 4–5.

104. Thomas Dublin, *Transforming Women's Work: New England Lives in the Industrial Revolution* (Ithaca, N.Y.: Cornell University Press, 1994) 11.

105. Laurel Thatcher Ulrich, "'A Friendly Neighbor': Social Dimensions of Daily Work in Northern Colonial New England," *Feminist Studies* 6.2 (1980): 403.

106. Bluestone and Harrison 67–69.

107. Folbre, Leighton, and Roderick 297; see also Bluestone and Harrison 69.

108. Wallace and Rothschild 24–27. See also Bluestone and Harrison 72–78, citing U.S. House of Representatives, Committee on Small Business, *Conglomerate Mergers—Their Effects on Small Business and Local Communities*, 96th Cong., 2d sess., report no. 96–1147, 2 October 1980, 10. Bluestone and Harrison cite examples of plant closings, the concomitant loss of the corporation's taxes on a local economy, and the tax burden that is shifted to local homeowners and the town's remaining small businesses.

109. For examples of how local and state governments lure businesses through tax incentives, low-cost financing, and other inducements, see Browne and Sims 67–68.

110. Bluestone and Harrison posit this contradiction between capital and community in their introduction; see esp. 19–21.

111. Staughton Lynd, *The Fight Against Shutdowns: Youngstown's Steel Mill Closings* (San Pedro: Singlejack Books, 1982) 166, quoting "Proceedings Had Before the Honorable Thomas D. Lambros . . . on Thursday, February 28, 1980," 11–12.

112. Lynd 176, quoting 492 F.Supp. at 10.

113. Browne and Sims 70–72.

114. For details on local, national, and international strategies, see Browne and Sims 53–92.

115. Bartlett and Steele, in *America: What Went Wrong?* make an especially strong case for the impact of U.S. legislation on the restructuring of corporate America. They call for a rewriting of "the government rulebook." They recommend enacting legislation that would eliminate such tax advantages, and suggest instead legislation that would reward corporations for investing in research and development within this country, as well as legislation that would encourage the creation of jobs that pay middle-class wages. See esp. 212–19.

116. I agree with Linda—that both the U.S. government and U.S. corporations are at fault here. In *Negotiating the Future*, Barry Bluestone suggests that labor and management must come to the negotiating table. My own perspective is that slowing or reversing the trend toward deindustrialization can only be accomplished if the U.S. government, U.S. corporations, and communities are all actively—if not collectively—addressing this issue. See Barry Bluestone and Irving Bluestone, *Negotiating the Future: A Labor Perspective on American Business* (New York: Basic Books, 1992).

117. William Greider, "Global Warning: Curbing the Free-Trade Freefall," *Nation*, 13–20 January 1997: 12. In his article, Greider proposes six "mutually reinforcing propositions" to redress global economic inequities, several of which seem particularly apt to this present discussion: "Bring the bottom up—raising wages on the low end as rapidly as possible—by requiring trading nations to honor labor rights" and "refocus national economic agendas on the priority of work and wages, rather than trade or multinational competitiveness, as the defining issue for domestic prosperity." He further points out that "if governments continue to be preoccupied with globalization and promotion of the free-market doctrine, then they must inevitably accept the consequences of deepening inequality and deterioration at home" (16–17). A "one world market" likewise implies a "one world labor force." See also William Greider, *One World, Ready or Not: The Manic Logic of Global Capitalism* (New York: Simon and Schuster, 1997). Jefferson Cowie's dissertation, "Rooted Workers and the Runaway Shop: Capital Migration and Social Change in the United States and Mexico, from the Great Depression to NAFTA" (University of North Carolina–Chapel Hill, 1996), offers an intriguing analysis of the challenges of transcending space and geographical distance between communities of workers across the globe. See esp. his final chapter, "The Distances in Between: Work, Community, and the Social Economy of Space" (323–62).

118. Bluestone and Harrison 20, quoting Paul Samuelson, "Aspects of Public Expenditure Theory," *Review of Economics and Statistics*, November 1958: 337.

119. Barringer lecture.

120. Bluestone, "Deindustrialization and Unemployment," 14–15. This study sounded intriguing, yet Bluestone did not provide further details here.

121. See Mary Ann Hinsdale, Helen M. Lewis, and S. Maxine Waller, *It Comes from the People: Community Development and Local Theology* (Philadelphia: Temple University Press, 1995).

122. Wallace and Rothschild 31.

123. Folbre, Leighton, and Roderick 305–6. For a detailed discussion of the history of Maine's plant closing law, see also 297–99.

124. Wallace and Rothschild 31. See *Fort Halifax Packing Co., Inc. v. Coyne*, 482 U.S. 1 (1987).

125. Rimer A13.

126. Rachel Carson, *Silent Spring* (Boston: Houghton Mifflin, 1962) 12.

Retelling the Story
of Linda Lord

ALICIA J. ROUVEROL

SC   *Would you say you were discontent, though, during the years you worked at Penobscot?*

LL   *I really wasn't happy. When I first went to work there, my hands were awful sore. They would swell up. You'd go home and you'd soak them and try to get so you could move them. And about when you got up in the morning so you could move your hands, you were back in there and you had to go through it again. Oh, it might take two or three months, and finally your hands get used to it. But it was a job. It was a fairly good paying job for around this area at that time. So, in some ways, I was content and not content.*

THIS BOOK IS NOT ONLY ABOUT LINDA LORD'S story of Penobscot's closing. It is also about oral history, why it matters, what it can tell us, and what it means for us as historians, folklorists, and documentarians seeking to make meaning of people's lives. Taking a close look at oral history narratives—at what they are actually saying—allows us to take people's stories at more than face value. Linda's critique of Penobscot Poultry, I believe, gets at the heart of some of the industry's real problems. And her ambivalence about the owners and the work itself says a great deal about the challenges, frustrations, and state of being both "content and not content" that most of us encounter daily. By exploring this book's methodology, we can better understand not only what oral history is but how collaboration can strengthen our work and alter what we present to the public. The very process of creating the manuscript forced us as authors to question the seemingly contradictory views Linda expressed, and this in turn encouraged us to work more closely with Linda to understand certain aspects of her story. What began as a book about the paradox surrounding Linda's story became a polyphonic, or multivoiced, dialogue expressing a range of perspectives and opinions.

SC   Linda, were you born in Brooks?

LL   No, I was born up in Waterville at the old sisters' hospital. But I've always lived here in Brooks. . . . After high school I went right into the hospital for an operation, and I wasn't supposed to work for a year; and come September, I got edgy and I started working a short time over at the [Unity] hatchery before I went down to the plant.

So begins Linda Lord's oral history testimony. As readers we might first ask: what is oral history, and what does it offer us? Scholars continue to grapple with issues of definition, purpose, and use. But it is generally agreed that oral history is both a product and a process. As a product, oral history usually takes the form of tapes and transcripts, which are used as a source for understanding the past. As a process, oral history involves the collecting, usually by recorded interviews, of an individual's recollections or life history.

It could be said that the process of oral history is "as old as history itself," that it predates history.[1] Efforts to collect oral evidence in this country date back at least as far as the antebellum period, when abolitionists took down the stories of fugitive slaves and published their accounts. By the 1920s, black scholars seeking to overcome Reconstruction stereotypes began more systematic efforts at documenting black experience. And by the early 1930s, historians at Fisk and other southern universities had initiated projects to gather oral evidence. But the single most comprehensive effort in oral history took place under the auspices of the Works Progress Administration and later the Federal Writers Project during the Great Depression. Unemployed writers and journalists recorded more than 2,300 interviews with former slaves and with blacks and poor whites in southern rural areas.[2]

Yet it was only in 1948, when Allan Nevins started an oral history program at Columbia University, that oral history as an academic enterprise first began in this country.[3] Inspired by Nevins, interviewers began gathering oral histories for use in scholarly research. At first, they focused on recording the histories of famous men. But with the rise of social history in the 1970s, scholars began to use oral history to gather the histories of men and women in all walks of life, seeking to recapture the experiences of—and give voice to—those who have traditionally been excluded from the historical record.

Recently scholars have begun to see oral history as more than historical data, more than the stories of the disenfranchised: it is also a kind of talk in which we all participate.[4] Recollection is part of all our lives. It is how we sift through and re-create our past, how we struggle to find words to capture our present, how we imagine our future. Is it really "history"? Is it really "past"? In weaving our stories, the boundaries between past and present often blur, as do those between our own story and the community whose stories we relate. To call Linda's testimony "personal narrative" puts the emphasis on her unique experience as an individual. To use the term "folk history," at the other end of the spectrum, highlights the storied experiences common to her cultural group.[5] We might think of Linda's oral history as encompassing both her personal narrative and collective memories and experiences.[6]

Oral history can also be seen as an act, a performance, or a communicative event in which we all engage. We tell our own stories—performing ourselves—within the changing contexts of our world. In reading oral history narratives, then, we might look closely not only at what the speaker says but at *how* she says it, at forms of self-presentation. This performance approach to oral history reminds us that stories are told in settings that include both performer and audience within a larger social and cultural context. By its very presence (or imagined presence), the audience shapes the performance, and the larger environment invariably influences how and in what ways the stories are told.[7] This leads us to some critical questions: To what extent are our narratives structured (or limited) by the communities and cultures in which we live?

Hatchery near Unity, Maine.

And in what ways do personal narratives support or challenge the traditional values and social confines of our worlds?[8]

How Linda tells her stories, then, is very much a part of her story. Throughout her oral history, she speaks of her work and of her relationship to her coworkers and her employers in what initially appear to be paradoxical statements. "I was content and not content," Linda said, describing how she felt about working at Penobscot Poultry. And it is this dialectic—in which contradictions are revealed and synthesized (or not synthesized, as the case may be)—which provides the central tension in Linda's story.

Sifting through another's life story is no simple task. As scholars, we are drawn to see oral history narrative as a window on the past, as another source of historical information to be used in making the generalizations standard to the study of history. Even more tempting is to perceive oral history as a direct link to the past, seemingly untainted by the interpretation of historians. But oral history sits at neither end of these extremes. "In their rememberings are their truths," Studs Terkel comments in regard to the people interviewed in *Hard Times*.[9] And this brings us to the core issue in oral history: that of memory—historical and personal. Rather than sidestep this issue or apologize for it, as oral historians we should instead push it to the forefront, precisely because it highlights much of what we can learn from oral history. How does memory shape experience? What happens to experience en route to becoming history?[10] How is our identity altered through this process?[11] Of interest here is the construction and reconstruction of narratives. What we recount—what we include, what we leave out—both reflects and affects how we perceive (or present) ourselves. Stories are a means of telling others about our lives, but they are also a means by which to fashion our identities.[12] In studying narratives, then, we can learn not only how the teller shapes his or her identity but also how this process may be influenced by larger social and political forces.

The complexity of oral history narratives is precisely its value to us as scholars, for it is the individual stories uncovered through oral history that often challenge our historical generalizations.[13] To unravel an oral history narrative like Linda's, we might ask three questions: Who is speaking? What is she talking about? And what is she saying about it?[14]

Who is speaking? Although Linda Lord is speaking in these interviews, she is speaking about more than just her own experience: "Everybody's had problems that's been there [hanging poultry]. A lot of people have had warts come out on their hands because of handling chicken. A lot of people have had tendinitis, you know. That work is hard work down there." Linda presents us with other points of view and perspectives as she perceives them; she both chronicles events and interprets them, making them history. As listeners/readers, we enter her world—a world of social relationships, of worker/management interactions, of personal choice and individual action, threaded together into a single story.

What is she talking about? She speaks of the particular—what she has experienced and witnessed firsthand—and at the same time she evokes a larger overarching story of which her story is a part. To illustrate that larger picture ("that work is hard work down there"), for instance, she draws upon her own and her coworkers' encounters with blood poisoning.[15] She tells us not simply the details of blood poisoning (or the strike or the job search) but also what those details mean for her: the work is hard; the protective gear does not work properly; she took a more difficult job for better pay; she is self-supporting and has to look after herself. Her stories and statements build upon each other. At moments they even challenge each other, hinting at more complex stories, ideas, visions, and concerns. Taken together, these seemingly disparate threads suggest how she conceptualizes her reality, makes order of her experience, and creates meaning in her life.[16]

What is she saying? What, in the largest sense, is Linda Lord telling us? She states that if she had not fought for the settlement on the accident, she would never have gotten it; that for her and her fellow workers the strike was a failure; that she could not attend the job retraining classes in part because she needed to look after her ailing mother. What Linda says about her personal experiences at Penobscot is highly political, whether or not she intended it to be.[17] And her testimony is political in another sense. Through examining oral history testimony, we can discover not only how an individual constructs her world but also how she has been encouraged to perceive the world around her.[18]

SC   When you folks were out on strike, what were George Lewis's reasons for not being able to give the union what they were asking for?

LL   The major reason was what it cost to raise birds here. You see, it cost a lot more up here than it did down South. So you can't give the people as much money, really. I mean, he claimed he had a margin that he had to go by. He knew what he could and couldn't do—and if we went for higher wages and stuff, there was no way that he could keep running and make ends meet and make money.

At one moment, Linda defends Penobscot's owners; at the next, she acknowledges the company's mismanagement or its inadequate or unfair policies:

CC Did they follow you around and watch you work? . . .
LL Sure. They watched the birds to see how they were bled out and if you were doing your job. Or they would try some dirty deal to see what they could get away with . . . try to take your time away, or cheat you out of it. Just give you a hassle, you know. But they didn't get away with much with me. Because when I figured that I was in the right, I went all the way. . . . I don't know how many times I threatened to get OSHA [Occupational Safety and Health Administration] in there and close that place down, if they didn't get some of the things to make my job easier—or just get off my back.

Do Linda's shifts in tone and statement represent contradictions? Is she inconsistent in her attitudes toward management, able to fight for her rights but unable to imagine a world in which workers' needs and rights might counterbalance management's self-interest? At one moment, Linda acquiesces to the prevailing attitudes ("You can't give the people as much money, really"); at the next, she challenges the status quo ("I don't know how many times I threatened to get OSHA in there"). These shifts reflect not self-contradiction but paradox, revealing how she, like most of us, simultaneously adapts to and struggles against her circumstances.

Linda Lord's narrative, then, is more than just her "story," more than a way of making meaning in her life. Her narrative points to a wider network of power relations and serves as a reminder of who she can—and cannot—be.[19] Her ambivalence toward Penobscot Poultry and its owners may reflect what labor historians call "divided consciousness," in which people consent with a complex mixture of resistance and resignation to the dominant culture.[20] For some historians, such consciousness leads to passivity and undercuts political action. Increasingly, however, scholars have countered this analysis, claiming that most subordinate groups seldom show either overt defiance of—or complete compliance to—those in power. Instead, their political actions often take the form of hidden stories: political critiques couched in rumor, gossip, metaphors, euphemisms, and folktales. And through such statements, those who do not hold formal positions of power often manage to voice their criticism, making a public story of their discontent and generating an ongoing, if muted, political dialogue.[21]

Linda's oral testimony brings to light one such hidden story. The day Penobscot Poultry closed—and Linda called Steve and Cedric to her table and began to tell them of her experiences in the plant—she initiated what we now understand to be, among other things, a political dialogue couched in the form of oral history.

So when Linda says, "I was content and not content" about her work at Penobscot, she speaks on many levels. We hear her struggle to balance a range of needs and desires with the limitations of her circumstances—a balancing act in which we all engage. We also hear what may be her divided consciousness, and through her testimony we witness a hidden story emerging into the public domain.[22]

In sharp contrast, when Carolyn Chute rails against the powers that be in her essay "Faces in the Hands"—and mocks the Maine work ethic—we see her refusing compliance altogether. Her story is far from hidden; it is in fact very public. Both Mainers, both hard workers, Linda Lord and Carolyn Chute may hold very different visions of the worker and her world, but they share this struggle against the constraints of their circumstances. And that is what links their respective stories.

Yet another similarity lies in the *very act of telling*. As performance, telling cannot be separated from action.[23] On this ground alone, both Linda's and Carolyn's narratives can be seen as political acts.[24] They are political precisely because they demand an audience. Carolyn, with her insistent tone, makes us listen to her story. Linda, calling Steve and Cedric to her table at Rollie's Cafe, makes them—and now you—her willing listeners. Through this process, the experience of the teller comes to belong also to the listener.[25] As Linda's and Carolyn's struggles become our own, we must ask ourselves to what extent we, too, are "content and not content" and what such ambivalence implies.

Telling (or Retelling) Her Story

This book presents the story of the closing of Penobscot Poultry as told by Linda Lord—and as retold by a host of coauthors. As readers we should ask critical questions of this or any documentary book: What is the role of the photographer/fieldworker/editor in retelling the interviewee's oral history? How do the documentarians shape the primary materials (the original recorded interviews and, later, the "raw" transcripts)? What does this say for the final product? And underlying all of these questions, *whose* story is being told?

Paradoxically, this book both *is* and *is not* Linda's story. It is polyphonic, a simultaneous expression of those who helped shape the product along the way: Linda Lord, Cedric Chatterley, Steve Cole, Carolyn Chute, and myself. The result is a dialogue—at times melodic, at times dissonant—from which emerges many stories. Linda's and Carolyn's voices, at least, are readily discernible; Cedric's, Steve's, and mine are less so. Yet we three have shaped this book in critical and very specific ways. By explaining this process, we bring our voices more fully into the dialogue, so that it becomes clear to the reader just who is speaking, how, and (most important) why.

How did we go about editing the transcripts? What decisions did we make and why? As much as possible, we wanted to adhere to the original interviews and to keep the narrative flow in the order it occurred, alongside the linear flow of the chickens moving through the plant (as shown in the photographs). We decided to include the questions not only to provide context for Linda's comments but also to remind the reader that he or she is reading *an interview*. This is not simply Linda "telling her own story." She is answering questions posed by Cedric and Steve—who are not plant workers, not Mainers, but men from very different walks of life. There is a dynamic interchange going on here, and to deny it or to avoid its implications not only falsifies the situation but gives the illusion that this narrative represents a fixed and static state of mind. It doesn't. Linda's comments reflected her opinions at the time, which may or may not have shifted in response to the changing particularities of the situation. And, of course, there is the issue of what she did *not* say in the interview, what never

Bayview Street in Belfast, Maine. (Penobscot Poultry is located in the center of the photograph.) Winter 1988.

emerged in the telling, or what might have emerged had Steve, Cedric, and I posed different questions.

We shaped the interview further when we began the editing process. The details of this process, usually kept sequestered in the hearts and minds of ethnographers, tell us a great deal not only about the difficulties of editing oral history narratives but, more important, about how narratives can "fight back" from the editing table, resisting our well-meaning alterations.[26] Our first such encounter occurred at the close of the March 1, 1988, interview, in editing the portion of the text that referred to Linda's loss of sight in her right eye. Our efforts to move the text to another section, to consolidate the material thematically, did not seem to work. We opted finally to leave Linda's story about her accident exactly where it appeared in the interview, precisely because the order in which Linda told her story seemed significant.[27] That Linda did not mention this incident earlier may have been due to her assumptions about what Steve and Cedric wanted to hear. But her prior reticence on the subject also tells us something about Linda, about her tendency to understate her own difficulties. As readers, when we stumble on the narrative describing the injury, we learn almost by accident how profoundly this experience affected Linda's health and her future work capacity.

Another encounter with the text "fighting back" occurred when we edited the later interviews. These interviews seemed less densely packed with information, less dramatic than the first interview, which had taken place not long after the closing.[28] Initially, we pared them down more tightly because the detail seemed overwhelming—and perhaps boring for the reader. In the end, we opted to include some of this detail because the loose, almost aimless quality of the interviews seemed to reflect Linda's experience at that moment. As readers, when we encounter the listlessness in that portion of Linda's narrative, we realize just how much unemployment affected her. Linda herself said that she was bored—after all, she was out of work, essentially for the first time in her life—and the narrative reflects that lack of energy and the sense of disconnection often accompanying job loss.

Linda's text "fought back" most dramatically when we tried to create the story as a whole. We leaned toward including mainly those portions of the text that tied her story together, that gave it coherence. We were similarly tempted to exclude those portions that we did not immediately like or agree with (for instance, her stance on unions). But our job was not to find within Linda's testimony our own perspective but to discover hers. In editing those portions of the text pertaining to unions and the rights of workers, we had to surrender to what the text—to what Linda—really said. As readers, we learn of Linda's positive and negative experiences with the union, which in turn tell us about the ways in which the union at once helped and failed her.

By surrendering to the text and letting go of the need to create an altogether cohesive story, we found the central story of our book. In our earlier edit for the exhibit text, we had focused on those aspects of Linda's experiences which were consistent. Only later, in reviewing the transcripts for the book, did we discover what seemed to be Linda's conflicting viewpoints. At one moment, she makes pointed comments about how the Lewises could have paid more; at the next, she insists that they treated her well. Yet both of these perspectives toward management drove her experiences there. Had we edited out these seemingly contradictory comments—simply because these did not fit our need to tell a coherent narrative—we would have misrepresented her story, or we would have missed her story altogether.

Finally, we also chose to retain the repetitions that came up in her narrative: her ailing mother, her experience as a self-supporting woman, her family's involvement in poultry. These were key to what mattered to Linda, to how she perceived her own experience.[29] At the same time, we also had to acknowledge the limits of even the most patient reader. It has been said that "people talk in spirals but read in lines."[30] We kept the first interview with Linda virtually intact, but the later interviews contained far too many "spirals." We opted to delete redundancies that did not introduce new or critical information or that did not seem to represent layers of recollection or uncovered memory.[31] We faced yet another editing challenge when we tried to incorporate the project's final interview into the narrative (an interview I conducted with Linda five years later, for very different purposes). We chose not to interedit the interview with the earlier material but to add it to the sequence of interview excerpts, despite the fact that it differed in tone, content, and style. We edited out much of the exchange about the book project and instead opted to leave in only those portions that show how Linda's perceptions had—and had not—changed over time.

Yet regardless of how we or other editors treat oral history transcripts at the editing table, the very process of oral history inevitably results in a kind of "retelling" of the story. Linda spoke the words, but Steve and Cedric guided the questions. Linda worked in the blood tunnel, sought subsequent work, and participated in community events, but Cedric framed these photographic images. And finally, Linda's narrative—although we kept it essentially intact—is *not* verbatim; Cedric and I shaped it the moment we included certain things and excluded others. As a result, the story reflects not only Linda's words and impressions but also the lens through which Cedric, Steve, and I perceive her world. Although our goal is to tell another's story, our own story is never fully out of the picture. Editing oral history text reminds us that objectivity is not only a myth but a deception.

Consider Steve's interviewing style, which included leading and often very pointed questions, especially in the first interview. (Mine were more pointed still, as I challenged her to consider some of my perspectives.) Although generally not recommended practice among oral historians, this style was particularly effective with Linda, yielding precisely the information Steve was after. In much the same fashion, Cedric's perception of the plant as "mechanized death" surely shaped the images he shot. How Cedric and I both perceived the plant's demise is reflected in how we edited the text and placed it beside the photographs. I now see the many ways in which we interedited the photographs and text—intentionally and unintentionally—to tell a story of contradictions. By using such strategies, Cedric and I may well have heightened the theme of paradox within this book. Consciously (and, I'm sure, unconsciously) we framed this story with a privileged eye, privileged in the sense that we assumed, as most of us do when we undertake this work, a level of authority in making such selections—rightly or wrongly.[32]

It was in the process of writing the book's introduction that I began to realize we had made some fundamental and perhaps questionable assumptions about Linda's story. At the urging of folklorist Glenn Hinson, I decided to take our analysis back to Linda, who by this time (five years later) had become a friend and colleague on the project.

In our taped conversation, I asked Linda two fundamental questions regarding her work at Penobscot. I wanted to understand her motivations for taking the job, and I also wondered if we had misunderstood her comment, "I was content and not content," which had become the book's unifying theme. As a folklorist, I had assumed that Linda had taken the job at Penobscot primarily because of her family's link to the industry—a common assumption in our discipline and a perspective Cedric and I had firmly held throughout the project. Linda insisted that, while she was familiar with chickens through her family's poultry work, economic need caused her to take the job at Penobscot. Linda's comments forced me to relinquish my more romantic view of her family's farming background and encouraged me to look more closely at the role of economics (or class) and gender in her work choices.[33] At the same time, our discussion of her statement, "I was content and not content," clarified my questions surrounding her seemingly paradoxical feelings toward her work. Her response reinforced my assessment that being "content and not content" did not reflect "divided consciousness" but rather a realistic understanding of her life experience. And what seemed at first to be paradoxical comments did *not* reflect dichotomous thinking.[34] Linda's seemingly contradictory perspectives were in fact integrated.[35]

Linda's honest responses to our analysis forced me to reconsider assumptions we had made about her work at Penobscot, but more importantly they influenced and altered what I now see in her story and how we have presented her narrative in the book. Where previously her commitment to family seemed central to her narrative, now it became clear that Linda chose to stay in Maine not simply because of family ties but because of strong roots to community and her abiding sense of place and home. Our engaged discussion forced me continually to reassess our analysis and also to take responsibility for the claims we were making about her life.

Our ongoing dialogue continues to inform my scholarship and to challenge my understanding of oral history, reminding me that it is—and should be—a collaborative process from start to finish.[36] As Michael Frisch has pointed out, we have to engage the power dimensions of this enterprise.[37] If we are truly to "share authority," we have to make ourselves accessible, available, and to some extent vulnerable to the individuals whom and with whom we study. If we are to do history from "the bottom up," as many social historians and oral historians have tried to do, we need to invite our participants to share in the process, not simply as colleagues but as coauthors of our work. We need not agree with their interpretations and analyses in the end, but I do feel we have the obligation to present their interpretations alongside our own.[38] Making history, to me, means making room for those outside the academy whose expertise lies not only in their learned (or schooled) experience but in their lived experience.

Collaborative oral history is one means by which we can "share authority." In the process, it also forces us to take a different kind of responsibility for the stories we tell. As ethnographers and authors, we are both vehicles for the interviewee's story and constructors of that story. It has been argued that the stories we retell often reflect issues and dilemmas that matter to us, in our own lives and cultures.[39] I couldn't agree more. I have been struck again and again by the parallels between myself and the individuals whose stories I have documented.[40] In the process of completing this book, I read Carol Stack's *Call to Home*, which has recently brought the theme of migration— of leaving and returning home—to national attention. Stack has written about the migration of African Americans returning to the South, about individuals returning to their homes to craft their lives anew.[41] Linda Lord's story, it struck me, is *all about home*—but about someone who was determined to stay. I was struck also by the irony that all of the coauthors of this book had chosen to leave our respective homes. If Linda's narrative about home and community resonates for you, too, then perhaps part of a collective story is being told here as well.

But it is Linda's seemingly paradoxical comment—"I was content and not content"—that I suspect will resonate most for readers. My final interview with Linda confirmed the theme of paradox and its centrality to her story. But our ongoing discussions made clear that Linda's "content and not content" predicament did *not* reveal an internal split—in Linda or in any of us. In a recent telephone conversation, as she detailed the factors influencing her decision to remain in her community, the multiple reasons behind Linda's decision to work at Penobscot and to stay in her home community became all the more apparent. Her testimony reminds us that a *range of factors* were at play here: economics, gender, rural values, family dynamics, commitment to home, commitment to family, among others. Her words ("I was content and not content") imply paradox, but her story (what she actually tells us throughout the narrative) implies polyphony, containing multiple perspectives simultaneously.[42]

The more we worked with Linda's narrative, the more I began to understand that Linda's experiences at Penobscot and thereafter were not black-and-white, either/or situations and did not in fact reflect dichotomous thinking, the kind of thinking that might paralyze Linda or any of us and make complex social and economic developments—such as industrial decline—seem insurmountable.

I am convinced that by acknowledging our own multiple perspectives and accepting the tension of that apparent paradox we can begin to open up to more creative responses to our circumstances, so that even something as vast as "deindustrialization" is no longer beyond the scope of our influence.[43] Yet how can we negotiate cooperatively the future of our industries and our communities? How can labor and management reach across the great divide that separates their polar camps? How can we recognize our interdependence, so that we can construct policies that serve both business and the people who devote their lives to those businesses? Each of these questions, as I have posed them, is constructed as "either/or," polar circumstances. Moving beyond that polarity and recognizing instead the multiple and overlapping interests of both parties may well be a more effective strategy. We might ask instead: what are our common ends? How can we further those shared ends? And how can we negotiate and compromise where those needs differ or depart? Linda Lord's ability to embrace all aspects of her experience, her willingness to acknowledge those conflicting needs and desires, concerns and interests, might well be an example for us all.

What began as a book about paradox, then, has increasingly become a book about polyphony and on multiple levels. We tell Linda's story from a range of perspectives, through a variety of mediums, offering multiple reflections on what her experience at Penobscot was about and on what plant closure means for working people like Linda Lord. At the same time, Linda's narrative itself is polyphonic, which suggests that all of us share such multiple threads and multiple identities. And common ground is easier to attain when we understand our shared commonalities. The process of collaborative oral history has reminded me of the potential for finding points of connection and intersection, even when we assume a lack of shared experience: for as the project progressed and Linda and I shared not just reflections on the manuscript but on our own lives, I began to see the parallels, the similarities between us, despite the differences in our respective worlds. Conversation across class lines, race lines, gender, culture, and community can begin to happen when we understand that each of us is made up of these multiple selves. We begin to realize, as Carolyn Chute did in her piece, that conversation *is* possible between herself and a pastel-shirt engineer. And if conversation, as she suggests, happens only between diplomatic powers, then it behooves us all to start owning our own power in those interchanges. Linda owned hers with Cedric and Steve the minute she began to engage with them in this project and even later as she and I moved on to have conversations and exchanges of our own.

What this project taught me was that dialogue is key. By presenting the range of Linda's experience at Penobscot—her appreciation of her employers, as well as her anger at their unjust behavior, we had hoped to bring all sides to dialogue. But I'm thinking here also of dialogue on other levels, not just on the written page: *internal* dialogues that we have within ourselves, the kind of countering, differing polyphonic threads that riddle Linda Lord's narrative, and how these might become *external* dialogues: conversations and exchanges, acknowledging what we share and don't share as workers, as plant owners, as oral historians, as colleagues. Change is possible, I believe, through such dialogues. We tell our stories to save our lives, it has been said.[44] I think we need to tell our stories, with all of their seeming contradictions, to one another and begin to listen—both for where our stories resonate and for where they

Linda on her three-wheeled motorcycle in downtown Brooks, Maine. Summer 1994.

collide. No one gains through silencing the voices of others or by avoiding hearing what we do not want to hear. I hope this project stimulates further dialogue: about workers, about plant closure, about who profits, when and why, from capital flight; about communities, how we can help sustain them; about businesses, how they can thrive and how we can help maintain them; about oral history (collaborative and otherwise), what its strengths are and what its limitations seem to be; about multiple and shared identities, our commonalities as well as our differences, about what we share and what we don't, what we can and cannot understand about one another.[45]

We set out, so many years ago now, to try to tell Linda Lord's story and the story of what had happened to Penobscot Poultry. Now, as I write these last sentences, I realize that Linda's narrative—especially those portions that we initially didn't want to hear—is what took us on this remarkable journey. There is more here, I'm sure, that we have missed. We invite you as readers to join us in this process of exploring the words and life of this extraordinary individual. We invite you to think about what it means to be "content and not content" (and to have such feelings simultaneously), what it means to move beyond such dichotomies to a broader sense of ourselves, a more complicated and difficult understanding of who we are. My hope is that Linda Lord's story will challenge you, as it has me. I hope that it will make you reflect on how you are "content and not content," that it will make you do as she did, the day she hailed Steve and Cedric to her table: act on that understanding.

Notes

1. Louis Starr, "Oral History," *Oral History: An Interdisciplinary Anthology*, ed. David K. Dunaway and Willa K. Baum (Nashville: American Association for State and Local History, 1984) 4. Paul Thompson makes a similar point, noting that oral history was "the *first* kind of history." See Thompson, *The Voice of the Past* (Oxford: Oxford University Press, 1988) 22.

2. James West Davidson and Mark Hamilton Lytle, "The View from the Bottom Rail," *After the Fact: The Art of Historical Detection*, vol. 2 (New York: Knopf, 1986) 186–87. See also Louis Starr 7.

3. Louis Starr 4.

4. Samuel Schrager, "What Is Social in Oral History?" *International Journal of Oral History* 4.2 (1983): 76.

5. Schrager 77.

6. In *The Way of All the Earth: Experiments in Truth and Religion* (New York: Macmillan, 1972), John S. Dunne states this concept from another vantage point: "There are two basic ways, we could say, in which a life may be considered: as a series of events and as the life of someone. When it is considered as the life of someone, then its story appears to be a tale which could be told of no one else, a unique tale from which no conclusions could be drawn about other lives or about time as a whole. When it is considered as a series of events, on the other hand, then its story appears to be a tale of things and situations which could occur in other lives too, a tale which could throw light on the entire course of human events" (135).

7. Kristin M. Langellier, "Personal Narratives: Perspectives on Theory and Research," *Text and Performance Quarterly* 9 (1989): 255. See also Richard Bauman and Charles L. Briggs, "Poetics and Performance as Critical Perspectives on Language and Social Life," *Annual Review of Anthropology* 19 (1990): 66–67.

8. Langellier 255–56.

9. Studs Terkel, *Hard Times: An Oral History of the Great Depression* (New York: Pantheon Books, 1970) 3.

10. Michael H. Frisch, "Oral History and *Hard Times*," *A Shared Authority: Essays on the Craft and Meaning of Oral and Public History* (Albany: State University of New York Press, 1990) 9–11.

11. Joan W. Scott, "Multiculturalism and the Politics of Identity," *Bulletin of the Conference Group on Women's History* 23.5 (1992): 10–11. See also Joan Alcoff, "Cultural Feminism versus Post-Structuralism: The Identity Crisis in Feminist Theory," *Signs* 13 (1988): 425. For a critique of the term "experience," see Joan W. Scott, "Experience," *Feminists Theorize the Political*, ed. Judith Butler and Joan W. Scott (New York: Routledge, 1992) 22–40.

12. See George C. Rosenwald, introduction to *Storied Lives: The Cultural Politics of Self-Understanding*, ed. George C. Rosenwald and Richard L. Ochberg (New Haven, Conn.: Yale University Press, 1992) 1. See also Sandra Dolby Stahl, *Literary Folkloristics and the Personal Narrative* (Bloomington: Indiana University Press, 1989) 21.

13. Steven Biel, "The Left and Public Memory," *Reviews in American History* 23 (1995): 704–9.

14. Frisch 10–11.

15. Schrager 92.

16. Schrager 95; see also Frisch 13.

17. For a discussion of the personal narrative as political praxis, see Langellier 266–71.

18. Frisch 11.

19. Langellier 267.

20. Leon Fink, "The New Labor History and the Powers of Historical Pessimism: Consensus, Hegemony, and the Case of the Knights of Labor," *Journal of American History* 75 (1988): 125–26. See also T. J. Jackson Lears, "The Concept of Cultural Hegemony: Problems and Possibilities," *American Historical Review* 90 (1985): 570.

21. James C. Scott uses the terms "hidden transcript" and "public transcript" to describe this process. See Scott, *Domination and the Arts of Resistance: Hidden Transcripts* (New Haven: Yale University Press, 1990) 136–38.

22. Through the exhibit and now this book project, we have tried to bring Linda Lord's story—this hidden transcript (literally and figuratively)—into wider circulation.

23. Judith Modell, "The Performance of Talk: Interviewing Birthparents and Adoptees," *International Journal of Oral History* 9 (1988): 23.

24. Edward M. Bruner, "Ethnography as Narrative," *The Anthropology of Experience*, ed. Victor W. Turner and Edward M. Bruner (Urbana: University of Illinois Press, 1986) 144.

25. Modell 17.

26. For one of the few examples of the editing process made public, see Michael Frisch's chapter, "Preparing Interview Transcripts for Documentary Publication: A Line-by-Line Illustration of the Editing Process," in his book *A Shared Authority*, 81–146. Dell Hymes also spoke of texts "fighting back" in a paper he delivered, "Theory, Performance, and Interpretation," at the American Folklore Society meeting, Pittsburgh, October 19, 1996.

27. At the close of the interview, after they had shut off the tape recorder, Steve, Linda, and Cedric began to discuss job-related accidents in other settings. Cedric mentioned that he had witnessed an eye loss accident while working in the oil fields, which spurred Linda to tell how she had lost the sight in her eye. Cedric turned on his tape recorder and caught her in midsentence.

28. It is not uncommon for the first interview to include more substantial information, since the interviewee and interviewer are usually trying to cover a lot of ground. Then, as the two parties get more acquainted, the subsequent interviews often become less formal and the material covered tends to fill in the story around the edges.

29. Editors frequently choose to edit and move text substantially (and we did so liberally for the original exhibit text). We are not suggesting that oral history interviews should not be altered. We are only advocating that the editing process should be organic to the material and to the goals of the project.

30. Michael Frisch heard this comment from someone at a conference, but its actual source is unknown. I discovered a similar notion in Paul Thompson's *Voice of the Past*, which may be the original source: "Written language is grammatically elaborate, linear, spare, objective and analytical in manner, precise yet abundantly rich in vocabulary. Speech on the other hand is usually grammatically primitive, full of redundancies and back-loops, empathetic and subjective, tentative, repeatedly returning to the same words and catchphrases" (243).

31. Aside from deletions of repetition, in general, when we edited the text we did so minimally (i.e., deleting false starts and extraneous expressions, such as "you know" and "like").

32. Such assumption of authority has recently come under critique in the fields of anthropology, folklore, and history. Increasingly, ethnographers have begun to acknowledge that fieldwork is a communicative interaction with the interviewee, involving not only shared time and space but also shared authority. See Dwight Conquergood, "Rethinking Ethnography: Towards a Critical Cultural Politics," *Communication Monographs* 58 (1991): 183. See also Michael Frisch, *A Shared Authority*, xv–xxiv. In recent years, the field of anthropology has experienced a "crisis in representation," in which ethnographers have begun to question their role in the field. See George E. Marcus and Michael M. J. Fischer, *Anthropology as Cultural Critique: An Experimental Moment in the Human Sciences* (Chicago: University of Chicago Press, 1986). Gone are the days when the ethnographer assumed that he or she could study a community and then present a written text—an "objective" scientific study—of the "Other's" culture. Today the fieldworker no longer attempts to be an objective observer but rather strives to "understand human conduct as it unfolds through time and in relation to its meanings for the actors." See Renato Rosaldo, *Culture and Truth: The Remaking of Social Analysis* (Boston: Beacon, 1989) 37. There is now both a willingness to share in the balance of power and an understanding that this is essential to the fieldwork endeavor. Recent trends in reflexive anthropology (in which the fieldworker acknowledges his or her influence as a fieldworker) and in reciprocal ethnography (in which the fieldworker encourages the response and participation of the interviewee) attempts to shift this balance of power even further toward the individual or community with whom one works. The ultimate goal, I believe, is collaborative ethnography, in which the interviewee is engaged in a dialogue with the fieldworker, and both are in dialogue with the text.

33. Collaborative oral history does not mean that we abandon our own stance, that we lose our "critical edge" as scholars. I still feel that Linda's family history and her early exposure to poultry were fundamental to her decision to enter poultry processing. This project and other occupational folklife projects have led me to believe that people often elect to "do" what they "know." Linda's stance on this issue did not completely change my own but rather broadened it, forcing me to consider the myriad factors at work here, and thereby enriching the story we finally told.

34. Elsa Barkley Brown comments that "rather than standing as 'contradictory opposites,'" these seemingly contradictory parts "become 'complementary, unsynthesized, unified wholes.' This is what Chikwenye Okonjo Ogunyemi refers to as 'the dynamism of wholeness.'" See Brown, "Womanist Consciousness: Maggie Lena Walker and the Independent Order of Saint Luke," *Signs* 14 (Spring 1989): 218, quoting Johnella E. Butler, *Black Studies: Pedagogy and Revolution: A Study of Afro-American Studies and the Liberal Arts Tradition Through the Discipline of Afro-American Literature* (Washington, D.C.: University Press of America, 1981) esp. 96–102.

35. Alicia J. Rouverol, "Paradox and Polyphony in 'I Was Content and Not Content': The Closing of Penobscot Poultry and the Story of Linda Lord: An Ethnography in Process," master's thesis, University of North Carolina–Chapel Hill, 1995.

36. It should be noted that collaboration isn't as easy as it sounds. Our initial efforts to collaborate with Linda were not terribly successful. Although we asked Linda to review the edited text and photographs and give us her feedback—both on the original exhibit and on the manuscript—she never changed a word of our work. It was "fine," she said. Yet the operative word here is "our work," because by virtue of our years of working on the project, the materials, it seemed, had become increasingly "ours" rather than Linda's. In fact, when we discussed our impending book contract, she always referred to the book as Cedric's and mine, despite our efforts to the contrary (and despite the fact that she, too, would share in the royalties). Ruth Behar had a similar response from Esperanza, a Mesquite woman whose story she gathered, translated, and carried across the U.S.–Mexican border. See Ruth Behar, *Translated Woman* (Boston: Beacon Press, 1993), 231–46, for a discussion of the power dimensions of their relationship.

I'm convinced that the power dimensions of our relationship with Linda Lord only began to shift after we had worked with her for a number of years. And, in terms of my own relationship with her, I noticed a substantive change after I began to share more of myself in our phone conversations, as I moved beyond documenting her story to sharing mine. Linda became more open—and not only about the work itself but also about her feelings about us, her interviewers. She now tells a hilarious story of her initial reaction to meeting Steve and Cedric.

37. Frisch, *A Shared Authority.* See esp. xx–xxiii and part 3, "A Shared Authority: Scholarship, Audience, and Public Presentation," 179–263.

38. See Elaine J. Lawless, *Holy Women, Wholly Women: Sharing Ministries of Wholeness Through Life Stories and Reciprocal Ethnography* (Philadelphia: University of Pennsylvania Press, 1993). In her study, Lawless engaged the women ministers she interviewed in her process of analysis. She calls this technique not "collaborative ethnography" but "reciprocal ethnography": "This new approach, which I consider to be inherently feminist and humanistic, takes 'reflexive anthropology' one step further by foregrounding dialogues as a process in understanding and knowledge retrieval. The approach is feminist because it insists on a denial of hierarchical constructs that place the scholar at some apex of knowledge and understanding and her 'subjects' in some inferior, less knowledgeable position. This approach seeks to privilege no voice over another and relies on dialogues as the key to understanding and illumination" (5).

39. See James Clifford's critique of *Nisa: The Life and Words of a !Kung Woman* in his article, "On Ethnographic Allegory," *Writing Culture: The Poetics and Politics of Ethnography,* ed. James Clifford and George E. Marcus (Berkeley: University of California Press, 1986) 103–9.

40. In "Paradox and Polyphony," I mention the parallels between Linda Lord and myself—how we are in some ways mirror opposites of one another, but how our differences also point up key similarities (103–5). Ruth Behar makes a similar point in *Translated Woman;* see esp. "The Biography in the Shadow," 320–42.

41. Carol Stack, *Call to Home: African Americans Reclaim the Rural South* (New York: Basic Books, 1996). Thomas Dublin and Walter Licht are currently working on a historical study of deindustrialization in the Anthracite region. They, too, have found the theme of migration (relocating for the purposes of work) and the desire of some families to stay put to be significant in the oral histories they are conducting. Dublin and Licht presented some of their findings in "Gender and Deindustrialization: The View from the Anthracite Region of Pennsylvania," which they presented at the Tenth Berkshire Conference on the History of Women in June 1996. In "Work and Deindustrialization in the Anthracite Region of Pennsylvania: A Gendered View," the paper they delivered at the 1996 Oral History Association Conference later that year, the topic of migration seemed more prominent still.

42. In "Paradox and Polyphony," I argue that "Linda's text alone is composed of simultaneous threads that blend together to tell not one story but a multitude of stories" (67).

43. Psychologist Linda Schierse Leonard comments, "Rather, it is living in the polarity, the multiplicity of different perceptions, and allowing the paradox of tension in our being, that opens up the creative." Philosopher Phyllis Kevevan argues that "it is precisely in this situation that new and better beliefs can emerge." See Linda Schierse Leonard, *Witness to the Fire: Creativity and the Veil of Addiction* (Boston: Shambhala, 1989), 221. See Phyllis Kenevan, "Nietzsche and the Creative Consciousness," *Man and World* (The Hague: Martinus Nijhoff, 1982) 388. Kenevan's complete quotation is as follows: "If one resists the 'intellectual corruption' stemming from the need to simplify and attends to the polarity, the result is not simply chaos, but a fertile sort of disorder; for it becomes closed off through systematic limiting beliefs. Even though there may be a vertigo of multiplicity and especially of contradictions, yet it is precisely in this situation that new and better beliefs can emerge. The creative potential is activated out of these open possibilities." I would argue further that belief is at the basis of our understanding, so that without changing our beliefs, fundamental change is not possible.

44. Jacquelyn Dowd Hall, "Partial Truths," *Signs* 14 (1989): 911.

45. Jefferson Cowie made a similar point in the paper he delivered at the Tenth Berkshire Conference on the History of Women, "Gender and Globalization in Comparative Perspective: RCA in Memphis, 1964–1971." He commented that in a time of increased recognition of our differences—across cultures, across the globe, across race/class/gender lines—it is increasingly imperative that we begin to find points of intersection and commonality.

Epilogue

STEPHEN A. COLE

November 1996, Brooks, Maine

EARLY IN THE SECOND WEEK OF DEER SEASON, I met Linda Lord for breakfast at Gallagher's Galley. It had been nearly eight years since Cedric Chatterley and I first interviewed her there. We learned from Linda much later that even though her home was a stone's throw from the restaurant, she had chosen a public place for our conversation in case we were a couple of shady characters. That story always makes for a good laugh now.

This time we traded news about Linda's dogs and my two young daughters, commiserated over our mutual need for snow tires, and commented on the wet summer and November's unseasonable cold. Linda had taken this week off to get some hunting in, and if the cold had any value, it was to get the deer up and moving. Around the coffee, French toast, and corned beef hash, we also talked of the Frye Mountain Band, the country group in which Linda is the drummer. My family had seen the band playing on a flatbed truck in Belfast's summer parade. The group had won the Mayor's Trophy. This month they were playing a holiday benefit and open rehearsal every Wednesday night out at Candy's on Route 137.

Thinking of our first talk at this breakfast place so long ago, when Penobscot Poultry had just closed, I asked Linda a question taken from Ronald Reagan: Are you better off now than you were at Penobscot? I wasn't prepared for the answer. "About the same," she replied. Crowe Rope had been sold about a year ago—one investor was a former Maine governor—and the struggling business had cut costs and consolidated. The upshot was that Linda and other plant workers took a pay cut, lost their health insurance, but kept their jobs. We left the subject there.

If Linda's employment hasn't changed much, has anything changed? What of Belfast, once the "Broiler Capital of the World"? Linda sees it as a city trying to attract tourists but thinks it should attract more industry, more employers like Penobscot Frozen Foods and Stinson's fish cannery. The hundreds of Waldo County people who work best with their hands need opportunities. The buzz in Belfast these days is industry—the service industry. Belfast has become an unexpected microcosm of recent American economic history. Out on the Route 1 bypass is the gleaming MBNA complex, a bit of suburban office park plunked down in one of New England's most rural regions. MBNA is a credit card bank, and its several hundred Belfast workers

133

market and service MasterCard accounts. The firm's presence heralds for some a turning point in the prospects and character of what was once a decidedly working-class community. In an act that nearly transcends irony, MBNA has given the city funds for the purchase and demolition of the empty Penobscot Poultry plant. A committee of citizens is now working out how the resulting public property should be used. Whatever the use, perhaps the site should include—as one resident has suggested—a monument to Penobscot Poultry's workers.

CEDRIC N. CHATTERLEY received a bachelor of science in sociology from Utah State University and a master of fine arts in photography from Southern Illinois University Carbondale. His photography has been supported by the National Endowment for the Arts and state and humanities agencies in Illinois, Maine, North Carolina, and South Dakota.

ALICIA J. ROUVEROL is a folklorist and a research associate at the Southern Oral History Program, University of North Carolina at Chapel Hill. She is a graduate of the University of Maine and the University of North Carolina Curriculum in Folklore and former associate director of the Northeast Archives of Folklore and Oral History. Her field research projects have culminated in exhibits, performances, video-documentaries, and articles.

STEPHEN A. COLE lives in Belfast, Maine, with his wife, Lindy Gifford, and daughters Phoebe and Eliza. He is a graduate of Brown University in American civilization and the University of Massachusetts at Amherst in regional planning. Cole is on the staff of Coastal Enterprises, Inc., a community development corporation based in Wiscasset, Maine.

I Was Content and Not Content
was designed by gary gore and edited by elaine otto
with production supervised by barb beaird.
The text was composed in 12-point adobe jenson by kyle lake,
and the book was printed and bound by
thomson-shore in dexter, michigan.